The financial system today

Eric E. Rowley

Manchester University Press

Copyright © Eric E. Rowley 1987

Published by Manchester University Press,
Oxford Road, Manchester M13 9PL, UK

Distributed exclusively in the USA and Canada by
St. Martin's Press Inc.,
175 Fifth Avenue, New York 10010, USA

British Library cataloguing in publication data
Rowley, Eric E.
 The financial system today.
 1. Finance—Great Britain
 I. Title
 332′.0941   HG186.G7

Library of Congress cataloging in publication data applied for

ISBN 0 7190 1494 8 *paperback*

Typeset in Great Britain
by Alan Sutton Publishing

Printed in Great Britain
by Biddles Ltd, Guildford and King's Lynn

The financial
system today

Contents

Acknowledgements

I would like to thank the Financial Times, the Wall Street Journal Europe and Sotheby's for permission to quote from their publications. Extracts from articles in the Employment Gazette are reproduced with the permission of the Controller of Her Majesty's Stationery Office. I am grateful to them all.

Such material from the 'real world' is invaluable as illustrations of the application of statistical formulae. Statistical summaries exist to interpret the world around us and only really come alive when applied to real data.

Introduction

The topics covered in this book arise out of courses of lectures given annually by the author in the programme of the Department of Extra Mural Studies at the University of Manchester.

The aim of these courses and hence of the book is to provide coverage of those topics and statistics that appear frequently in the media and that relate to various aspects of the financial system today.

It covers the recent developments in indices and markets. Attention is given to describing and analysing the changes in nature and structure of the economic relationships that lie behind the published statistics and that generate a demand for new indices to capture and track the new situations.

The book aims to inject an interest by going into some considerable detail on the construction and uses of the various statistics covered. These constructions are not difficult to follow but are mostly avoided in the superficial surface-skating of the popular investment magazines that touch on some of the areas discussed in this book. It fills part of the wide gap between the 'popular' magazines and advanced statistical textbooks.

The emphasis is entirely practical. It seeks to answer the fundamental questions that may be asked of any statistic. How is it calculated? Why is it important? What does it signify when it moves by a given percentage? What use is made of it? By whom is it used? For what purposes?

Much published data is not fully accessible to most people because of its technical nature. The popularity of courses dealing with such material suggests a need for a volume such as this.

Many textbooks go from the general to the particular, often

leaving the student to make any particular desired application. This text rather goes the other way, from the particular, the student is left to generalise to further possible applications of the concept in question. The author's teaching experience suggests that this is a fruitful approach for many students.

Overall, the approach is to attempt to understand the financial system through published information; subsequently to link the instrument or institution described to other relevant worlds–of economic policy, manufacturing industry and personal incomes.

The book would be an excellent complement to existing economics texts which stress the general, the timeless and the theoretical at the expense of the particular, the contemporary and the real.

The book will be of interest to many different groups of readers. It will be of value to pupils and students for GCSE and A level examinations in economics in schools, sixth form colleges, technical colleges and certain university examinations in economics and financial subjects. Much of the material covered has been piloted on groups of such students. Some of the topics have formed part of courses provided for teachers of economics and will be of interest to those generally who are looking for an updating and perhaps coverage of material omitted from their own undergraduate courses.

Students on trade union and social studies courses who need to know about the use of indices as part of bargaining strategies or to understand how poverty and welfare may be in part quantitatively assessed will find the relevant chapters useful. Trainee stockbrokers and banking students will find much of the material directly relevant to their needs as will amateur investors and portfolio managers who want to know more about the key statistics that measure market performance. The material will also interest those who simply wish to know more about the flood of statistics that pour from the newspapers, radio and television.

The book goes some way to meeting those requirements of school and college teaching of economics selected as important by a joint committee of those interested in the teaching of the subject.[1] Their report stressed the importance of dealing with 'problems of measuring change; measurement of price changes; measurement of real changes' and 'understanding the general characteristics and limitations of the main sources of date'.[2]

Notes

1 *The Teaching of Economics in Schools*, Report of a Joint Committee of the Royal Economic Society, the Association of University Teachers of Economics and the Economics Association, Macmillan, 1973.
2 ibid, p. 15.

Chapter One

British government securities

The government's need to borrow

Examination of the financial pages of the newspapers will reveal the closing prices of the previous day's trading on the London Stock Exchange. A significant section of the prices reported relates to the trading in British government securities, or, as it is more colloquially and generally known, the gilt-edged market.

The British government has a need to borrow. This need arises because its revenue from taxation is insufficient to cover its expenditure. The government has been a systematic net borrower in peacetime only since the end of the Second World War. Prior to this period, governments had aimed, wartime exigencies apart, to balance the budget, that is, to ensure that their expenditure was equal to their income derived from taxation. The post-1945 commitment to nationalisation, the development of the Welfare State, the costs of substantial defence expenditure and the then new economic theories of J. M. Keynes[1] ensured that there would be a continuing need to borrow in peacetime.

The excess of public sector expenditure over income derived from taxation and the sale of goods and services is known as the Public Sector Borrowing Requirement (PSBR).[2] It currently stands at around £10,000,000,000. The total of outstanding borrowings is called the National Debt.

The Conservative government elected in 1979 has tried as part of its Medium Term Financial Strategy to reduce these borrowing requirements. It has published a target for the PSBR of £7,000,000,000 by the financial year 1989/90, a reduction of some 30%.[3] The figures remain large for the foreseeable future and indicate a continuing need for the government to raise relatively large sums of money by the issue of gilt-edged securities.

The ability of the government to borrow is greatly facilitated by the existence of the Stock Exchange. If one lends to the government by buying, say Treasury Stock 1988 or Exchequer 12% 2013/2017, then the money lent will not be repaid until 1988 in the former case and some time between 2013 and 2017 in the case of the latter.

Money lent to the government may be needed by the lender at any time for many reasons. The Stock Market operates as a market bringing buyers and sellers together. It enables those who have lent to the government to sell their entitlement to interest payments and ultimate repayment to another person. Nowadays, sales and purchases may either be made through a broker using the Stock Exchange with the transfer of ownership being registered on the Bank of England's Stock Register held in the National Debt Office of the Bank or through the National Savings Register at Lytham St. Annes. The latter is attractive to the small investor because the associated costs of acquiring gilts in this way are lower and the interest payments are made gross, that is, without tax being deducted at the prevailing standard rate. The disadvantage is that 'up to the minute' price quotations are not available because postal application has to be made. The advantage of buying through a broker is his continuous contact with the market.

The prices recorded in the financial press relating to British government securities thus show the prices at which ownership is changing hands. Actually they show mid-market prices: an average of the closing buying and selling prices. An investor will be faced with a buying price higher than the price at which he could sell the same security. The printed price is an average of the two. More detailed information on buying and selling prices is to be found on the *Stock Exchange Daily List*.

What is gilt-edged about British government securities?

The words 'gilt-edged' or simply 'gilts' to describe British government securities are interesting; they imply a unique degree of security of the borrower to the lender. Lending to the government is more secure, in some sense, than lending to any other individual or institution. The power of the government to levy taxation and raise further loans stands as security behind the debt. The state cannot go bankrupt and fail to meet its financial obligations in the same way as an individual. It must not, however, be thought that this security extends to the full protection of capital and interest.

J. Shield Nicholson wrote nearly seventy years ago that it is

irrelevant to speak of the security of the British Government . . . old Consols are practically unsaleable at the official price, 35 below par. The interest covenanted for is no doubt quite secure, so far the guarantee of the British Government is perfect–but the capital value becomes less with every rise in the outside rate of interest. It would indeed be a national misfortune if small people are induced to put their savings into the War Loan under the idea that they can at any time draw out the money intact with the accrued interest. The War Loan is an excellent investment for the small person but the market price will be subject to variation and should be allowed for.[4]

This was written as a commentary on the urging of small people to buy 5% War Loan 1927–1947 by means of 25p vouchers and £5 bonds. The years before the First World War had experienced a long period of stable interest rates. Rates had risen during the war as a response to the increased borrowing requirements of the government and foreign creditors' worries about their war-threatened debtor. The rise in the War Loan rate from 3.5 to 5.0% had depressed the market value of the earlier loan by £30 per nominal £100 lent, that is, by $100 \ (1-(3.5/5.0))$.[5]

Further comment on gilt-edging

The following story is an old one but it is instructive and still forms a topic of conversation when lending to the government by buying gilts is discussed.

The Great War of 1914–18 had been financed in part by the issue in January 1917 of 5% War Loan, redeemable at 100 between 1929 and 1947. The government announced the redemption date as 1 December 1932 with investors offered either cash or reinvestment in a replacement issue also called War Loan but carrying a lower coupon rate of 3.5%. The latter is still extant today.

Whereas the initial issue in 1917 carried a redemption date, the replacement 3.5% was an undated stock. The subsequent loss in value of this issue due to the general rise in the level and structure of interest rates and inflation has frequently led to criticism of the government for allegedly breaking faith with investors by allowing this to happen.

It raises the general question of the responsibility of government towards holders of the National Debt in a period of rising interest rates and hence of capital losses. War Loan 3.5% is referred to particularly in these criticisms because of the patriotic urging to subscribe to the issue in the first place and the equally strong urgings in 1932 to accept the lower coupon to help the country during the financial crisis.

The general feeling expressed by those who feel that the government has a special responsibility to holders of War Loan is that the patriotic fervour of those who contributed to the financing of the First World War should have been matched by a grateful government with at least the protection that a dated stock would have offered.

These comments and caveats about the security of investments in gilt-edged securities written about a particular type of gilt issued during the Great War apply to gilts generally today. What is protected, what is gilt-edged, is the coupon rate, the annual interest payment expressed as a percentage of the issue price or nominal value of the stock. The capital value is not protected on a day-to-day basis and is determined by trends in interest rates subsequent to the issue of a particular gilt. At redemption, for a dated non-index-linked stock, the nominal sum lent will be repaid. This known redemption value will exercise an increasingly powerful influence towards the end of the life of a stock, but interest rate considerations will be paramount in the early years after the issue of a dated stock. Writing in 1986, a gilt redeemable in 2021 is 35 years from redemption. Although this 'pull to redemption' effect ensures that the 2021 redemption date exercises a progressively stronger pull on the market price of the gilt as time goes by, over the next several years, relative interest rates will dominate the determination of relative prices. The existence of this 'pull' effect will dominate the price determination in the last few years before redemption. Just before redemption, the market will ensure that the price of the stock is very close to its redemption value but the government's guarantee is discharged only at redemption and not before.

On non-index-linked gilts, the real value of the money lent to the government at the issue date may be very different from the real value repaid at redemption, that is, the redemption 'guarantee' aspect of the gilt relates to the nominal, not the real amounts lent. The value in real terms of such redeemed borrowings depends upon the inflation rates over the life of the gilt.

The six extant undated stocks were all issued prior to 1950. This is not without significance! The Conservative government of 1951 reactivated monetary policy with its associated fluctuations in interest rates and hence to fluctuating prices and yields on British government securities. The progressive dismantling of postwar price controls and rationing allowed pent-up inflationary pressures to appear and the 30 years from 1950 to 1980 was a period of rising levels of inflation. These developments highlighted the need for some protection of capital values: putting more'gilt' into the 'gilt-edged' securities. This has largely been achieved in two ways. Firstly, by the issue of Exchequer Stock with a low coupon rate and at a substantial discount on the ultimate redemption value and secondly, by the issue of index-linked stocks.

Gilt prices and accrued interest

One certainty of gilts that has been discussed above is the date and amount of the next and all subsequent interest payments. If, for example, a 4% Consol is bought on 1 May, then it is known that the next dividend payment of £2 is due on 1 August, that is, £2 due in 92 days' time. Any gilt will be more attractive, other things being equal, the nearer the next dividend date it is traded. The price will rise towards the next dividend date by a predictable certain amount. In the present example, the 4% Consol pays an interest of £4 per annum in two payments of £2 each. This amounts to 400p per 365 days which amounts to 400p/365, equal to 1.096p per day. The price will thus be higher by this cumulative amount daily. The interest is paid every 6 months in arrears. If the gilt is sold, say $\frac{2}{3}$ of the way between dividend dates, then the seller has effectively been lending his money to the government for $\frac{2}{3}$ of the 6 months between dividend payments and the buyer for the remaining $\frac{1}{3}$, assuming he holds it until the next dividend date. Thus, of the next interest payment of £2 paid for a total waiting period of 6 months. $\frac{2}{3}(£2) = £1\frac{1}{3}$ is due to the seller and £$\frac{1}{3}$ to the buyer. This interest may be thought of as accumulating or accruing at the rate of 1.096p per day.

Quoted gilt prices may be printed to include or exclude these amounts of accrued interest, that is, the 4% Consol price on that particular day may include or exclude the £$1\frac{1}{3}$. Before 1 March 1986, gilt prices, except for those with less than 5 years to run to redemption, were quoted to include accrued interest. As from 1

March 1986, all gilt prices are shown excluding accrued interest.

The method of presenting price information does not affect the total to be paid when purchasing gilts but it might mislead. Any quoted price now needs to have accrued interest added to calculate the total payable.

Changes from 1 March 1986

Prior to 1 March 1986, accrued interest had to be calculated and deducted from quoted gilt prices before the yields could be checked. As prices are now quoted net of such interest, the printed price in the financial press is the appropriate denominator for yield calculations. Consider the following example (price quotation from *Financial Times*, 7 April 1986):

Treasury 13% 2000 dividend dates	Price	Interest yield	calculation
14.1 and 14.7	£128.75	10.10% =	13/128.75

Yields may simply be checked by dividing the coupon by the currently quoted price: (£13/£128.75) 100 in this example. Reading the rest of the information is easy. Names such as Treasury, Exchequer and Consol are ways of referring by name to a particular issue of gilts, that is, a particular act of borrowing by the government. The percentage coupon rate, 13% in this example, tells us the amount of interest per annum, £13 in this case, but as a percentage of the nominal value of the stock, £100 in this example. Yields are thus normally different from coupon rates because current prices differ from nominal values. The year 2000 tells us when the gilt will be redeemed, that is, when the government of the day will repay the nominal amounts borrowed.

Calculation of the accrued interest is still required as this will be added to the price paid by the purchaser and be received by the seller of the gilt. The contract note for the sale of the gilt will indicate not a price that is a composite of accrued interest and price but a division into these two elements. The itemised accrued interest will attract tax at the individual's highest marginal rate of tax if he is the seller. The price at which the gilt is sold, compared to the price paid, is the seller's capital gain or loss. Such gains are totally tax-free from July 1986.

A sale on 4 April would be a sale 79 days after the last dividend payment. The seller would have lent his money to the government for those 79 days and thus be entitled to an accrued interest total of £13(79/365) = £2.81p. Reference to Figure 1.1 should make the visualisation of this easier.

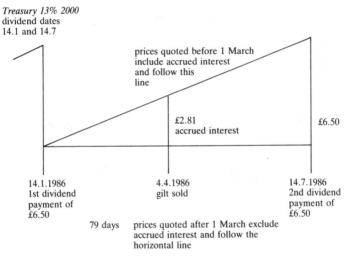

Treasury 13% 2000
dividend dates
14.1 and 14.7

prices quoted before 1 March include accrued interest and follow this line

£2.81
accrued interest

£6.50

14.1.1986
1st dividend
payment of
£6.50

4.4.1986
gilt sold

14.7.1986
2nd dividend
payment of
£6.50

79 days   prices quoted after 1 March exclude accrued interest and follow the horizontal line

Figure 1.1   Example of accrued interest

With similar price prior to 1 March 1986, the quoted price of this particular gilt would have been £128.75 + £2.81 = £131.56. Nothing fundamental has changed, only the method chosen to present the summary financial information relating to gilt-edged transactions.

The tax changes have been considerable. It is not now possible to engage in bond-washing. Prior to these changes, there were tax advantages in selling gilts with the next interest payment anticipated in the price, that is, including accrued interest rather than taking the interest as a dividend payment. This arose because interest accrued in the price of the gilt was treated as part of capital rather than income. More favourable rates of tax on capital gains meant that there were substantial tax advantages in this procedure. This has now changed. Interest payments from gilts, whether as dividend payments or as accrued interest, are now taxed as income.

Undated gilt yield calculations from 1 March 1986

An undated gilt is simply one for which there is no definite date set at which the original sums lent will be repaid. They are highly unlikely ever to be redeemed if only because they represent loans raised at coupon rates very much lower than ever seem likely to prevail in the future.

The *Financial Times* of 7 April 1986 carried the following information about two of the six extant undated stocks on a day in 1986:

Security	Dividend Dates	Price	Yield	calculation
Consol 2.5%	Jan. April July October	128.75xd	8.69%	$= £(2.5/28.75)100$
Consol 4.0%	February August	£44.75	8.94%	$= £(4.0/44.75)100$

For reasons discussed above, we would expect the coupon rate ratio (2.5/4.0) to be the same as the current price ratio (28.75/44.75). There is, however, a slight difference with the price ratio at 0.642 compared to 0.625 for the coupon ratio. Notice that the expectation that the ratios will be identical is an other-things-being-equal reasoning. Here other relevant considerations are not exactly equal.[6]

The 2.5% Consol is slightly overpriced at first sight in terms of ratio expectations and arises largely because the interest is paid four times a year compared to twice yearly for the 4.0% Consol. In a market with virtually a perfect flow of the relevant information, relative prices line up to accommodate and reflect such differences.

The price of 3.5% Conversion Stock is also 'out of line' because of the existence of a sinking fund. Some £935 million was issued between 1921 and 1927 and a sinking fund established to buy back 1% per 6 months of the amount outstanding when the price is £90 per £100 nominal or less. It is the buying by the authorities under the sinking fund provisions established under the terms and conditions of the original issue that causes the price to be higher and the yield lower than otherwise comparable stocks such as 3.5% War Loan.

Yields on redeemable gilts

The Treasury 13% 2000 gilt discussed above will be repaid in the year 2000. £100 will be paid to the then holders of the gilt compared to a price of £128.75 in April 1986. Thus, anyone buying at this price and holding until redemption will experience a capital loss of £28.75 over the 14 years to the end of the century. Consider the following information:

Treasury 13% 2000

Price	Redemption value	Rate of capital loss	Interest yield	Yield to redemption
£128.75	£100	0.89% per 6 months over the remaining 14 years	10.10%	9.21%

For dated stocks, a yield to redemption is calculated and published as well as the interest yield already discussed. The loss of £28.75 from the present price to the redemption value amounts to a semi-annualised rate (compounded 28 times over the 14 years to redemption) of 0.89%. This is deducted from the interest yield to give the yield to redemption which balances interest payments against capital losses. This relationship between interest yield and yield to redemption is typical of all gilts issued at higher coupon rates than those prevailing on current new issues of gilts. For relatively low coupon gilts, the yield to redemption is higher than the interest yields, meaning capital gains for those who buy now and either hold to redemption or benefit from the pull-to-redemption effect on the price already discussed.

Index-linked gilts

The last few years have seen a number or innovations in methods of financing the Public Sector Borrowing Requirement. The histori-

cally very high inflation rates in Britain during the 1970s highlighted
the lack of protection that gilt-edged securities provided for the real
value of investment funds. One of these innovations was the
introduction of index-linked (IL) gilts in March 1981, the first such
stock being a 2% IL Treasury Stock redeemable in 1996 that was
issued on 27 March of that year. Both the interest payments and the
capital value to be repaid at the redemption date were to rise in line
with inflation as measured by the Retail Prices Index.[7]

There are a number of reasons behind the issue of index-linked
gilts. The index-linking offers good protection against inflation as
both dividends and capital values are indexed. The stock can thus
be offered to the market at lower rates than would be possible
without the index-linking. Thus, if the government's monetary and
fiscal policies are successful in achieving the principal declared aim
of the Thatcher administration's Medium Term Financial Strategy
of controlling inflation down to low single figures, then these low
real rates will reduce the cost of servicing the National Debt. If the
government is unsuccessful and inflation rates rise to anything like
the nearly 30% rates of the seventies, then the cost of the
index-linking would significantly increase the cost of servicing the
National Debt.

Yields to redemption for these gilts cannot be calculated unless
an assumption is made about the inflation rate between the issue of
the stock and its redemption date. Therefore, looking back from the
redemption date, the yield to redemption historically calculated
may well be very different from the forward projections on specific
inflation rate assumptions made by the financial press. At the time
of writing, the *Financial Times* publishes two estimates of the yields
on index-linked stocks on assumption of 5% and 10% respectively.

The reader may expect, from the above discussion, that index-
linking both redemption values and dividend payments would
ensure that the gross real redemption yield of a 2% IL gilt would be
2% and that of a 2.5% gilt likewise 2.5%. This is not so, as
inspection of published yields shows that, although all index-linked
gilts have only to date been issued at either 2% or 2.5% coupons,
the real actual yields all differ from the coupon rates.[8]

The conditions summarised in Figure 1.2 would ensure that the
real yield to redemption of the stock remained at 2%. We would
also have to assume that the stock was traded continuously at a
price that lay on this line. This could only be achieved by having the

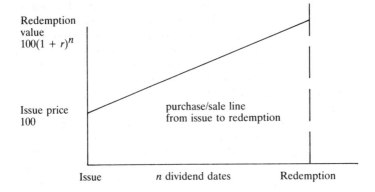

Figure 1.2 Hypothetical 2% index-linked stock

Bank of England continuously ready to buy and sell at this price. In that case, no one would sell the stock at a lower price and no one would have to purchase the stock at any higher price. Thus, the real return would always be 2%.

The indexing for these IL gilts begins with a base value of the Retail Prices Index (RPI) 8 months before the issue date and ends 8 months before redemption. This situation is illustrated in Figure 1.3.

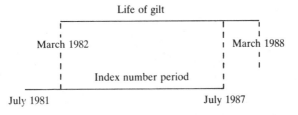

Figure 1.3 Treasury 2% IL 1988

The periods cannot be coterminous for two main reasons. Reference has already been made to the need to take into account accrued interest in calculations relating to gilt-edged securities. To do this, the next interest payment must be known. Continuous lagless indexing would make this impossible. Six months of the lag arises therefore from a need to know the next indexed dividend payment. The other 2 months allow for inevitable administrative delays in the calculation and publishing of any months RPI figure.

The lagged nature of the indexing will have no effect on the inflation protection afforded provided the inflation over the 'unprotected' last 8 months of the gilt's life is the same on average as the figure for the first 8 months of the indexing period. This would yield the same terminal sum as lagless indexing.

One major difficulty of working out an interest yield for IL gilts is that the future stream of dividend payments, apart from the next payment, is uncertain. They depend upon future and hence uncertain inflation rates. For this reason, interest yields are not shown for these gilts. Rather the problem is approached essentially as a cash flow analysis. It is known when payments will be made and an assumption about inflation will enable estimated rates of return to be calculated. The yields published in the *Financial Times*, for example, assume 10% and 5% respectively.

Let us assume an annual rate of inflation of 10% over the remaining life of the Treasury 2% IL Gilt 1988 and assume that it is now 30 March 1986. The next semi-annual dividend payment on 30

Table 1.1 Treasury IL 2% 1988: Calculation of the real return assuming 10% per annum inflation from 30 March 1986 until redemption on 30 March 1988

Price 30.3.86	Cash flow				
	Dividends				Capital Repayment
	30.9.1986	30.3.1987	30.9.87	30.3.88	30.3.88
£119⅛	£1.2780 certain	£1.3419	£1.4090	£1.4794	£147.9445
		£1.2780	£1.2780	£1.2780	£1.2780
		$\times\ 1.05$	$\times\ (1.05)^2$	$\times\ (1.05)^3$	$\times\ 100$ $\times\ (1.05)^3$

September 1986 will be £1.2780. This is known, as the relevant RPI ratio is 379.7/297.1 x £1, that is, Jan 1986 RPI/July 1981 RPI. The remaining payments to redemption in March 1988 have to be calculated and are shown in Table 1.1. A simplifying assumption that 10% per annum inflation equates to 5% per half-year has been made in the calculation thus ignoring the compounding effect that means that 5% per half-year yields slightly more than 10% per annum.

The question now is, what semi-annual rate of return does this projected cash flow represent on the price quoted? The arithmetic answer is that rate of discount at which the cash flow will equal the price, that is, r in the following equation:

$$119\tfrac{1}{8} = \frac{1.2780}{1 + r} + \frac{1.3419}{(1 + r)^2} + \frac{1.4090}{(1 + r)^3} + \frac{149.4239}{(1 + r)^4}$$

where r, the semi-annual nominal rate of return, is 6.9% close to an annualised rate of 13.8%. Deducting the assumed 10% rate of inflation leaves the real return at 3.8%. If the calculation is repeated with an assumed rate of inflation of 5% (semi-annual = 2.5%), the real return is shown to be higher at 4.6%

These calculations show that index-linked gilts are by no means a perfect inflation hedge. The real rate of return is itself dependent on the assumed inflation rate. Indeed, the lower the assumed rate of inflation, the higher the real rate of return on a given investment in IL gilts. It is debatable whether the procedure of assuming a constant inflation rate, as in the worked example, is better than perhaps a variable rate altered as forecasts change.

It may help to visualise geometrically what is calculated in the table in terms of the indexed capital sum: see Figure 1.4.

Another graph for the indexed interest payments could be drawn. This would be the same shape with a vertical scale 10^{-2} the scale in Figure 1.4. The vertical summation of the semi-annual values of both these diagrams beyond B provides the cash amounts in the formula above that are discounted back to the purchase price C to estimate the nominal return available on this particular gilt at this particular time.

Buying index-linked gilts is only one way of holding gilts that offer protection against inflation. Non-index-linked gilts can also

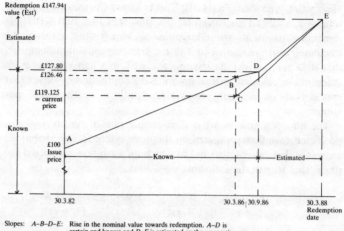

Slopes: *A–B–D–E*: Rise in the nominal value towards redemption. *A–D* is
                  certain and known and *D–E* is estimated on the assumption
                  of 10% p.a. inflation
        C–E: growth rate from the current price as at 30.3.1986 to the
                  estimated redemption value

Figure 1.4   Treasury 2% IL gilt: 6-year life March 1982 to March 1088;
indexing period RPI July 1981 to July 1987

offer this protection. A real rate of return for such non-index-linked
gilts may be estimated by deducting an estimate of the inflation rate
from the gross yield to redemption. The Treasury 13% 2000 gilt
considered above has a nominal gross yield to redemption of
9.21%. If inflation is expected at a rate of 5%, this would mean an
estimated real gross yield of 4.21%. Because of the uncertainties
about future inflation, it is not at all certain whether longish-term
inflation protection is likely, in the final outcome, to have been
better afforded by an investment now in IL gilts or non-indexed
alternatives.

Interest rate volatility and gilt futures

The last few years have been a period of widely fluctuating interest
rates. Associated with such movements has been an increase in
volatility. The corresponding changes in the capital values of
portfolios have caused problems for investors, fund managers and
corporate treasurers.

Such changes may be shown on a diagram as a series of yield curves. To obtain the information to draw such yield curves, we need to choose a number of gilts that are identical as far as possible in terms of the risk of default of the borrower, tax treatment, and marketability. If the yields on such gilts are then related to the number of years left to redemption, then curves are obtained as in Figure 1.5.

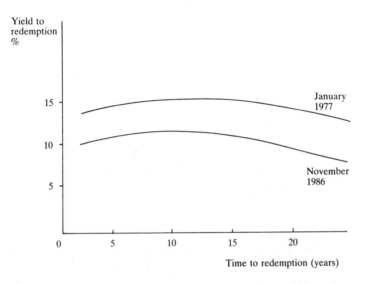

Figure 1.5　The yield curve: British government securities

Such yield curves move over time as those in the diagram show. Sometimes, the curves move sharply. They may also change shape with perhaps the short end moving quite markedly and the long end not at all.

We live in a financially very uncertain world. Which way will the yield curve move next? Forecasting is not such a well developed art that we can forecast with total confidence for next week, let alone for six months ahead.

The literature is strewn with articles indicating the imprecise state of the art as far as stock-market price forecasting is concerned.

The years from the early 1970s to the mid-1980s have been a period of interest rate volatility. This may be observed by inspecting the yield curve diagram (Figure 1.5) or simply by looking in the columns of the financial press at a range of coupon rates on listed gilts. These range from 15.5% Treasury issued in 1976 to 9.5% Treasury issued in 1982. This range of coupon rates implies something like a 60% price differential on the higher coupon-rate stock on interest rate considerations alone.

The decision to buy gilts may be effected only at a future date if cash flow considerations prevent immediate purchase at today's prices and yields. Thus, the prospective future purchaser is vulnerable to quite violent price and yield movements. To wait until the cash flow position allows the purchase to be effected may mean that the price has risen and the yield fallen. It is attractive to be able to 'lock in' at today's prices and yields. Even if prices fall and yields rise, the prospective purchaser will not know this in advance and may not be prepared to risk the probability of a favourable move when to do so also means carrying the risk of an unfavourable movement. Certainty at a known price and yield for the future purchase may be preferred.

Futures markets exist in part to provide certainty in an uncertain world. Commodity futures have existed for a long time but until recently there was no financial futures equivalent to the commodity futures markets.

As a manufacturer of chocolate, I can fix the price to be paid for my cocoa inputs by buying forward, that is, I fix the price per tonne and quantity to be supplied at that price now for delivery at a fixed future date. I thus have a firm price now on which I can base firmer estimates of product prices.

A similar possibility now exists in relation to financial futures to reduce gilt market uncertainties in the shape of the Twenty Year Interest Rate Contract traded on the London International Financial Futures Exchange (LIFFE).[9]

An investment fund manager or corporate treasurer may expect to make a future purchase of gilts but is concerned that between now and then prices will rise and yields fall. He may 'hedge' or protect his funds against this feared adverse movement by buying a notional LIFFE gilt-edged stock. This involves an outlay of £1,500 per £50,000 nominal stock purchased.[10] If he is correct and prices do rise, the sale of his futures contract will then enable him to buy the same nominal value of gilts as before the price rise and thus to 'lock in' to today's prices and yields.

There is an objection to this line of reasoning. In so far as the general expectation is that prices will rise, the expected extent of the rise will be discounted (taken into account) in setting the present price of the gilt futures, that is, futures prices are set now with reference to what the expected price trend into the future is expected to be. Thus futures prices will normally stand at some premium or discount in relationship to current prices depending upon what the market consensus is about future trends.

This argument suggests that the purchase of a financial future will be at a price that reflects market opinion about future trends. Thus, if a rise in price is expected, the futures contract price will be at a premium in relationship to current prices. On this view, the hedge or protection bought is against a price rise over and above that expected and generally, the certainty of a fixed price as an aid to fund management or corporate financial planning.

Thus, the existence of hedging instruments protects us against something absolutely awful happening in so far as it allows us to do at least as well as the general market consensus.

Reverse yield gap

Take any financial newspaper and look at the Stock Market closing prices of the previous day's trading. Look first at the yields on British government securities (gilts). At the time of writing, April 1986, a figure of around 9% would seem representative. Look next at the yields on equities, that is, on ordinary quoted company shares. An average yield of around 4% looks reasonably representative. The essential point is that there is a clear gap easily discernible by simple inspection between gilt and equity yields.

A gap between these yields is to be expected. If lending to the government through the purchase of gilts is more secure than lending to the private sector by the purchase of equities, then gilt yields should be lower than equity yields: there should be an adjustment for risk premium in equity yields. Simple inspection shows that the gap between the yields is the other way round, gilt yields are higher than equity yields and have been for a very long time.

What then is the possible explanation of this *reverse yield gap*.

The security of lending to the government is clearly more than offset by other factors. The explanation lies in the market evaluation of the relative merits of gilts and equities as investments in a period of inflation.

Locking in and being locked out!

From the calculations and discussions above, it should be clear that yields fall as gilt prices rise. If, anticipating trends correctly, one buys gilts ahead of such a change, one may enjoy a higher yield over a period in which the then currently available yields have fallen and also a capital gain when one's holdings are sold. One is said to have 'locked in' to current rates.

If one has anticipated incorrectly, and bought only to find that subsequently yields have risen and gilt prices fallen, one will be 'locked out' from the possibility of achieving the now higher returns.

The gilt options

Gilt options were introduced by the Stock Exchange in January 1985.[11] Buying gilts exposes one to the risks associated with interest rate movements and the options introduced allow one to hedge the risks associated with interest rate and associated price movements.

The options introduced (Table 1.2) are based on an actual gilt, Exchequer 10% 1989. The broad considerations applying to gilt options are those applying to the other options discussed above.

Table 1.2   Gilt options

Exchequer 10% 1989	Option exercise price	Feb 1985	May 1985	Aug 1985
Underlying share price = 94	94	$1\frac{1}{4}$	$^{22}/_{16}$	$2\ ^{9}/_{16}$
	96	$\frac{1}{2}$	$1\frac{1}{4}$	$1\ ^{23}/_{32}$
	98	$\frac{1}{8}$	$^{19}/_{32}$	$1\ ^{5}/_{32}$

Note: minimum movement = $\frac{1}{32}$ point
Source: *Financial Times*, 23 January 1985

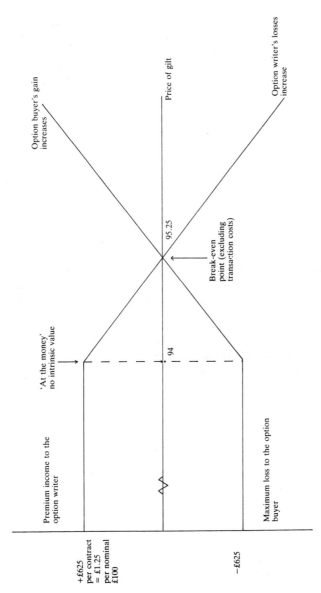

Figure 1.6 Exchequer 10% 1989: analysis of February 1985 Call Option Exercise Price 94 and Option Premium 1¼ on 23 January 1985

The information is read as follows. The February option exercise price of 94 means that £100 nominal of the stock may be acquired by exercising this particular call option for a price of £94. To acquire the right but not the obligation to exercise this particular option, a premium is payable per £100 nominal of £1.25 to keep the option open until the February expiry or £2 ¹⁄₁₆ per nominal £100 to keep this option exercise price available until the May 1985 expiry.

In the first example, this means that the two-stage process of acquiring the gilt in this way would cost a total of £95.25 per £100 nominal. This example is said to be 'at the money' that is, it has no 'intrinsic value'. This is market jargon for saying that the underlying stock price is equal to the particular option exercise price of £94. To make it worthwhile buying the actual stock this way would require an upwards movement in the market price of the gilt, that is, a fall in interest rates.

The contract size is £50,000 nominal. Thus the premium per contract is (£50,000/£100) £1.25 = £625. The total cost of acquiring the £50,000 nominal stock via an option contract which is subsequently exercised would be a total of £47,625.[12] See Figure 1.6.

As with other options, it is the fast moving premiums that attract traders or speculators. There is the usual traded option characteristic of relatively large premium changes in response to relatively small changes in the price of the underlying security. A 10 per cent or more change in premium would not be uncommon often for zero change in the price of the underlying stock. The other characteristic of these options is the very fast moving nature of the market. It is not a market to dabble in from afar; one needs close continuing contact with the market if one is to profitably exploit the traded nature of the option.

In summary, as for other options, the call option hedges the risk of a price rise and interest rate fall and a put option will hedge the opposite risk, a fall in price and a rise in the rate of interest.

Although this option is linked to a specific gilt, it will act as a more general hedge against changing prices and interest rates as interest rates tend to move together.

Notes

1   J. M. Keynes, *The General Theory of Employment, Interest and Money*, Macmillan, 1936. This book provided the economic reasoning and

intellectual justification for the post-1945 adoption of the unbalanced budget as part of the policy weapons available to government. It thus helped to ensure the permanent peacetime existence of a borrowing requirement.

2 The excess of government expenditure over taxation was previously known as the budget deficit. However, the term Public Sector Borrowing Requirement more accurately describes the sources of the excess of expenditure over income as the borrowing is required to cover a proportion of local authority expenditure, and the deficits of the nationalised industries as well as a part of the central government's own direct expenditure.

3 *Economic Progress Report*, Supplement 183, March–April 1986, p. 2, HM Treasury.

4 J. Shield-Nicholson, *War Finance*, p. 305, P. S. King & Son, London, 1918.

5 It is easy to see why this should be so. If an investor is buying gilts, he will, other things being equal, seek to maximise his return. Paying £70 for the right to receive £3.50 per annum gives the same return as paying £100 for the right to receive £5.00 per annum. Thus, the ratio of the interest rates (the coupon rates) at which the debt was originally issued determines the price ratios of the stocks. This is a first approximation holding strictly true for undated stocks only, that it, those without a set redemption date for the repayment of the original sum borrowed. This is extensively discussed later in the chapter.

6 Investors seeking to maximise the returns on their funds are responsible for this tendency, other things being equal, of coupon rate ratios to equal price ratios. If an investor can buy the right to receive £4.00 for an outlay of £44.75, then he will expect to pay, again other things equal, 0.625 of this amount (£28.75) to receive an amount of $0.625 \times 4 =$ £2.50.

7 J. Rutteford, 'Index-Linked Gilts', *National Westminster Bank Review*, November 1983.

8 *Index-Linked Government Stocks*, Bank of England, 1983.

9 *The Twenty Year Gilt Interest Rate Contract*, The London International Financial Futures Exchange, 1983.

10 This is an example of 'margin trading', that is, buying in effect against a relatively small deposit, thus economising on the use of 'owned funds'.

11 *The Gilt Options*, Stock Exchange, London, 1985.

12 £50,000 nominal would cost £0.94 × £50,000   = £47,000
Plus premium 500 × £1.25   =   625

                                                   £47,625

Chapter Two

Measuring share price changes

General problem

Share prices are continuously changing in both directions and by varying amounts. The general problem is how best to summarise the mass of data on the thousands of price changes taking place not only daily but continuously throughout the day.

Some averaging is clearly called for. An average price change will show the general direction of share price movements. How many share price changes should be averaged? Average the price changes of too few shares and we risk producing a figure that is representative of our chosen shares but totally unrepresentative of share price movements as a whole. Average all price movements and the result may be representative of market trends generally but may be too expensive or time-consuming in the data collection costs involved. Also, how often do we require to update the index? The present FT 30 Share Index[1] is updated every hour and the FTSE 100 Index[2] is maintained as a 'real-time' index updated on a minute-by-minute basis.[3]

Having decided what to average as representative of all share prices, how often and for what reasons are the constituents of the index to be altered? What sort of arithmetical procedure are we to use to 'average' our data?

Types and properties of certain means

When most people think of an average or the mean value of a set of price observations, they think of what statisticians call an *unweighted arithmetic mean*.

Table 2.1 Price change data

Share	Price (p) Day One	Price (p) Day Two	Price change
A	100	106	+ 6%
B	80	80	0%
C	130	128	−1.5%

Consider the three share price changes shown in Table 2.1 and the problem of averaging them. What is the average price change, given the individual share price changes in the table above?

The reader may quickly answer that it is $\frac{1}{3}(6 + 0 - 1.5)\% = 1.5\%$. As an answer to the question, what is the unweighted arithmetic mean, it is perfectly correct but there are other questions that may be asked that show this form of the average to be inadequate.

The unweighted arithmetic mean implicitly assumes that a given change in one of the share prices is no more or less important than the same change in the price of any other share, for example, a one per cent change in the price of share A in the table is as but no more important than a one per cent change in the prices of shares B and C. This may not be so and should not uncritically be accepted.

Firm A might be very large, employing thousands of people and with a market capitalisation of millions of pounds, whereas firm C might employ a few hundred only with a market capitalisation of a few hundred thousand pounds.

Table 2.2 Weighted price change data

Share (1)	Price changes from (2)	Market capitalisation (3)	Weight (4)	Price change (5) = (2)(4)
A	6%	£2m	0.57	3.42
B	0%	£1m	0.28	0.00
C	−1.5%	£0.5m	0.14	−0.21
		£3.5m	1.00	+3.21

The change in the price of firm A's shares might thus be more significant for the economy than a corresponding change in the price of firm C's shares. We may want our index to give more weight to firm A's shares than to firm B's and firm C's shares. A way of doing this is to weight the share price changes by the market capitalisations of the companies represented in the index. A revised set of calculations reflecting this discussion is set out in Table 2.2.

The average price change is now 3.21% More weight has been given to share A because of the greater market capitalisation of company A and its assumed greater significance in the economy. The price change of each share is now weighted according to the relative market capitalisation of the company. This is an example of a weighted mean and is the principle underlying the construction of the FTSE 100 Share Index introduced in January 1984.

In the example, before weighting, one-third of each share price change contributed to the overall average. After weighting, this is shifted so that 57% of the change in the price of share A, 28% of share B's price change and 14% of share C's price change contribute to the calculated average. Relative market capitalisations suggest themselves fairly readily as a logical basis for weighting the index but it is ultimately an arbitrary choice of procedure among a number of other possibilities such as measures of market dominance or the numbers of workers employed. The Standard and Poor's 500 Share Index in the United States, for example, weights by the relative numbers of shares outstanding.[4]

There is yet another way of averaging share price data. We may calculate a geometric mean of the individual share price changes.

At its simplest, an arithmetic mean is calculated by adding the n numbers and dividing by n to produce the mean value. A geometric mean involves finding the nth root of the product of the n numbers. For example, the geometric mean of the numbers 6, 3 and 2 is thus $3\sqrt{6.3.2.} = 3.304$, the cube root of the product of the three numbers. Calculated thus, the geometric mean would be useless for measuring share price changes. It cannot handle zeros and negative numbers; thus, it could not handle constant or falling prices. For business index purposes, and complex numbers apart, there is no point in even thinking about roots of negative products.

There is a way of organising the data so that a geometric mean may be calculated. This is shown in Table 2.3 for an unweighted arithmetic mean: the basis on which the FT 30 Share Index has been calculated for the half-century or so since its introduction on 1 July 1935.

Table 2.3 Calculation of a geometric mean

Share	Price (t)	Price ($t+1$)	Price ($t+1$) Price (t)	*log*
A	100	106	1.06	0.0253
B	80	80	1.00	0.0000
C	130	128	0.98	1.9912
			3	0.0165
				0.0055
			Antilog =	1.013

The method involves calculating a ratio of each price in period $t+1$ to its price in the previous period t. The arithmetic sum of the logs of these price ratios is the log of the product of the price ratios. The arithmetic mean of this sum is the log of the geometric mean. Using antilog tables, the geometric mean is thus obtained and shown to be 1.013 or a 1.3% increase in the average level of these share prices.

Table 2.3 shows a convenient method of evaluating

$$\sqrt[3]{(1.06 \times 1.00 \times 0.98)} = 1.013$$

The method is suitable for stock price changes and can handle negative, zero and positive changes. The method cannot handle a price that drops to zero, but this is not a practical problem. Neither can it handle negative prices but of course trading in shares is simply not going to take place at prices below zero. No one is actually going to pay a buyer to take shares off him nor is giving shares away at zero prices likely. If a price were to fall towards zero, something seriously wrong with the company would be indicated and trading probably suspended.[5] The company would then probably be replaced in the index by another 'more representative' share. Thus, this restriction on the range of values that the method can handle is of no practical significance.

During the discussion so far in this chapter, we have used three

different arithmetical procedures to average the same set of three
individual shares price changes. These are summarised below:

Summary of the calculations of average price changes

Unweighted arithmetic mean	1.5%
Weighted arithmetic mean	3.21%
Unweighted geometric mean	1.3%

The same data has been summarised in these three different ways to
illustrate the arithmetic underlying the construction of the most
common indices quoted and discussed in the financial media today.
No one method is more right than any other. The methods have
different properties that may make one more appropriate than the
others depending upon the particular purpose the analyst has in
mind.

FT 30 Share Index – Why the geometric mean?

It is interesting to consider why the geometric mean rather than the
arithmetic mean was chosen to form the basis of calculation of the
Financial Times 30 Share Index at its inception in 1935.

It was argued at the time[6] that there are two major advantages to
the use of the geometric mean: the facilitation of an alteration of the
base date of the index and the substitution of a new share for one
which has become unsuitable. The base date has not been altered in
the half-century since its introduction. There have, however, been
frequent alterations[7] to the base date of the weighted arithmetic
mean based Retail Price Index since its inception in 1914. As is
shown in summary form above, given data on the price changes
taking place in each time period, mean price changes can be
calculated either geometrically or arithmetically and converted to
an index with equal facility regardless of the year chosen as the base
period. The dropping of a share from the FT 30 Share Index
because it is no longer representative of the changing structure of
the British economy in favour of a 'more representative' ordinary
share is directly analogous to dropping an item from the Retail Price
Index because it has ceased to be a significant part of consumers'
retail expenditure.

A major academic force behind the adoption of the geometric mean was the English economist, William Stanley Jevons. In 1863, Jevons read a paper before the Statistical Society encapsulating his arguments in favour of the widespread use of the geometric mean for business indices.[8] It has been written of Jevons that 'he originated ideas which were capable of becoming the basis for long trains of systematic development'.[9] The appropriate average for the measurement of price changes was one of these and it is not fanciful to see the influence of the early works of Jevons on the choice of the geometric mean for the FT 30 Share Index some 70 years later. Certainly the views of Jevons helped to determine the fashionability of the geometric mean for indices of many sorts in the years after the Great War. This is particularly evident in the writings of A W Flux, a statistician much influenced by Jevons.[10]

Jevons's original use of the geometric mean was justified in his investigations of the likely effects of the (then) recent gold discoveries on the assumption that an increase in the supply of gold was likely to affect all other commodities in the same ratio. The mathematical properties of the geometric mean make it particularly suitable for averaging ratio changes.[11]

However, Jevon's original example was the averaging of a 100% increase in the price of corn and a 50% decrease in the price of cloves. The use of the geometric suggests a zero overall change in the price level, the 100% increase being just offset in the calculation by the 50% decrease. The use of the arithmetic mean would give more weight to the higher numerical price change and show an average price change overall of +25%.[12]

His choice of the geometric form was because the arithmetic mean would have the general result of 'greatly to exaggerate the prices that have risen at the expense of those which have fallen'.[11] This argument links to the reversibility criterion that is met by the geometric but not the arithmetic mean an argument of balance and symmetry. As a 100% increase in the price of a commodity can be fully offset by a subsequent 50% reduction from the higher level and a 50% reduction requires a subsequent 100% increase from the lower level to restore the initial price, it is in this restricted sense that we may think of 50% and 100% as equal. The geometric mean in effect weights these two percentages in the 'corn and cloves' example equally.

Replace 'corn and cloves' with two share price changes. If share

A rises by 100% and share B falls by 50%, are we really concerned with reversibility criteria? If we happen to have equal investments in A and B, then our portfolio will have increased by 25% in total value, not stayed constant. Thus, if we wish our index to more nearly track the portfolio value impact of changing share prices, the geometric form is at a marked disadvantage compared to the arithmetic and is one of the major reasons for the introduction in 1984 of the FTSE 100 Share Index.

Inspection of the summary on p. 26 shows the 'downward bias' of the geometric mean compared to the arithmetic, but only weakly so. This is because the percentage changes in the share prices are not too dissimilar. In the limiting case where all the commodity price changes percentage-wise are identical, the geometric mean value is equal to that calculated using the arithmetic form and the indices arrived at likewise numerically identical. Downward bias thus becomes more numerically significant the more disparate are the values being averaged. At the time of its introduction in 1935, this particular property of the geometric mean powerfully influenced its choice as the basis of calculation of the FT 30 Share Index.

One may think of share price changes as being determined by general economic and financial factors as well as those specific to each of the companies whose shares form the index. Examples of the former might include, for example, interest rate changes, the latest money supply figures and reported monthly trade flows. Factors specific to the company include profit for the year as revealed in the accounts, increased trading of the shares perhaps due to a takeover bid or particularly buoyant or depressed trading conditions in the inevitably narrow section of the economy in which one company operates.

It the purpose of the index is to reflect general movements in share prices rather than to be unduly sensitive to the effects on one or two share prices of special factors, then the downward bias of the geometric mean tends to remove the effects of factors causing share prices to change unequally because of special factors leaving the index to reflect those factors causing share prices to advance or fall more or less due to the operation of the same general factors.

Jevons's original view that gold supply changes would have approximately an equal percentage effect on all prices and that therefore this effect could be isolated from other particular price-influencing factors by using the geometric mean is similar to the argument developed above for the use of this form of the mean to measure general movements in share prices.

The geometric mean is much more useful in this respect as it damps extreme movements. An 'extreme movement' in a share price is one that is 'out of line' with general changes possibly caused by company-specific factors and not the general factors broadly affecting the whole economy that cause prices generally across the spectrum to move up or down.

There are other circumstances in which the last thing we would wish to do is damp an extreme price movement. In measuring 'cost of living' changes, it may be particularly important to allow a large single price change to be fully reflected in the index. This would be especially so if a particular commodity is considered an important budgetary item of those consumers whose 'costs of living' we are trying to express in index form. In this case, the weighted arithmetic mean discussed above is more appropriate. Here, relative price changes are emphasised as their relative importance suggests by a system of weighting chosen by studying consumers' budgets.

The discussion above illustrates that the mathematical properties of the geometric mean and the arithmetic means make them suitable for somewhat different measurement situations. They 'are all indirect attempts at the measurement of an elusive quantity'.[13] It is a question of choosing and interpreting index numbers given an understanding of the advantages, disadvantages and limitations of the alternative forms available.

The calculation of the FT 30 Share Index is set out in Table 2.4 between the closing prices for the thirty shares on 3 June 1985 and those prevailing on 4 June 1985. In practice, the calculation is done by computer but the mathematical procedures are set out below in the table.

The calculation shows an increase of 1.105% in the average level of share prices between these dates. Because of the 'downward bias' inherent in the geometric mean, a portfolio equally distributed between these thirty shares would have increased in value by somewhat more than the 1.105% calculated.

The index is not normally reported as having increased or decreased by a given percentage. It is normally reported as having risen or fallen by so many index points. Thus, having calculated the percentage change in the average level of prices, we need to convert it into a corresponding number of index points. The 1.105%

Table 2.4 The FT Share Index – worked example

Companies	Closing prices		Price relatives
	4.6.1985	3.6.1985	
Allied Lyons PLC	198	195	1.0154
Associated Dairies Group PLC	160	154	1.0390
Beecham Group PLC	385	380	1.0132
BICC PLC	230	230	1.0000
*Blue Circle Industries PLC	532	528	1.0076
The BOC Group PLC	310	309	1.0032
Boots PLC	187	184	1.0163
The British Petroleum Co. PLC	530	527	1.0057
British Telecommunations PLC	196	196	1.0000
BTR PLC	368	363	1.0138
Cadbury Schweppes PLC	158	157	1.0064
*Courtaulds PLC	142	141.5	1.0035
*The Distillers Co. PLC	295	298	0.9899
*The General Electric CO. PLC	186	184	1.0109
Glaxo Holdings PLC	1275	1275	1.0000
Grand Metropolitan PLC	303	305	0.9934
*Guest, Keen & Nettlefolds PLC	228	222	1.0270
Hanson Trust PLC	237	233	1.0172
*Hawker Siddeley Group PLC	430	429	1.0023
*Imperial Chemical Industries PLC	768	761	1.0092
*Imperial Group PLC	191	186	1.0269
Lucas Industries PLC	309	302	1.0269
Marks and Spencer PLC	137	136	1.0074
National Westminster Bank PLC	672	665	1.0105
Peninsular and Oriental Steam Navigation Co. PLC	360	360	1.0000
The Plessey Co. PLC	144	142	1.0141
*Tate and Lyle PLC	470	462	1.0173
Thorn EMI PLC	478	463	1.0324
Trusthouse Forte PLC	137	138	0.9928
*Vickers PLC	300	300	1.0000

Note: The geometric mean of this set of price changes is the 30th root of the product of the price relatives.

$$\sqrt[30]{(1.0154 \times 1.0390 \times \ldots \times 0.9928 \times 1.0000)}$$

$$= \quad \sqrt[30]{(1.3840)}$$

= 1.0110 This is a 1.1% increase in the average level of these 30 share prices from the closing prices on 3 June 1985 to closing prices the following day, 4 June 1985.

*Shares used in the index calculation from its inception

increase in share prices converts into 1.105 index points if we choose to define a base of 100 as at the close of business on 3 June 1985. The index would then rise from 100 to 101.105. The FT 30 Share Index, however, stood at 1010.7 at the close on that day. The 1.105% increase converts into an 11.1 index points increase to carry the index to a new level of 1021.8. It should thus be clear that the number of index points that the index moves between given points of time cannot really be given any significance unless we know the level from which the movement has taken place.

The calculation is set out in the way it would have been calculated before computers were available. The easy calculation of geometric means using logarithms was one reason that commended this method of averaging to Jevons.

Calculation by hand was probably a major reason for calculating the index initially only on a daily basis using closing prices. Electronic aids enable these calculations to be done more rapidly today and changes in the FT 30 Share Index were recorded on the hour, every hour during Stock Exchange trading hours as well as producing an index based on closing prices until July 1985. From 8 July 1985, the index has been calculated as a 'real-time' index: continuous updating every time the price of one of the constituent shares changes.[14]

The asterisk against certain share prices shows those shares whose prices form the basis of calculation of the index that have appeared since the beginning of the index on 1 July 1935. The companies introduced into the index at intervals since 1935 reflect changes in the structure of the economy. The changes reflect particularly the shift from manufacturing towards a more service-based economy.[15]

The index shows whether buying or selling pressures predominate overall in the market for the thirty shares and acts as a good proxy for the impact of supply and demand forces for traded shares generally.

Interpretation of index movements over time

In Figure 2.1 is displayed the behaviour over time of the FT 30 share index from its inception on the 1 July 1935 until May 1986. In that time the index rose from its base value of 100 to just over 900 and, over the next 2 years to 1986, to 1300. What interpretation are we to place on such time series information.

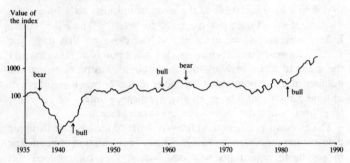

Note: The vertical scale is logarithmic. Thus 100 corresponds to 2 units on the vertical
       scale and 1000 corresponds to 3 units. This has the impact of reducing the visual
       impression of changes on the vertical scale.

Figure 2.1   FT 30 Share Index 1935–1986

It shows both trends and fluctuations around trends for this period of half a century. It shows that broadly the behaviour of stock market prices is such that periods in which prices are (fluctuations apart) rising are followed by periods in which the general trend is downwards, that is, 'bull' market conditions are followed by 'bear' markets. The term 'chartists' describes those analysts who believe that such timeseries data contain sufficient regularity in its behaviour that 'turning points' on the graph can be identified and made use of in making profitable share buying and selling decisions.

It does not mean that an equally balanced portfolio of thirty shares bought in 1935 and maintained in line with the changing composition of the index would in 1986 be worth some 13 times as much as in 1935. This is due to the 'downward' bias of the geometric form of the averaging process used. Such an investment would in fact be worth significantly more than that indicated by the index change. There is no information in the FT 30 Share Index that would enable us to know just precisely how much more. To know how much more such a portfolio would be worth, we would have had to maintain an index based on the arithmetic mean over this period.

The index has become a symbol with a general psychological interpretation attached to it quite remote from its inherent mathematical properties. Upward movements are thought of in some sense as 'good' and downward movements as 'bad'. One should beware of accepting uncritically value-loaded words such as these.

Why the FT 30 Share Index is unsuitable for the 1980s
The FT 30 Share Index was calculated hourly during business hours. the appearance of the latest hourly figure lagged the transactions it measured by up to one hour which was too long a lag for the information requirements of dealers in the new financial instruments introduced in May 1984. This objection was met by the introduction of continuous updating in July 1985.

Statistical fashion had also moved since 1935. By the 1980s, the weighted arithmetic mean was in favour as this form of averaging reflected the portfolio consequences of share price changes better than the geometric mean. Covering only 30 share price changes was also thought to be a drawback to relying solely on the FT 30 Share index and judgement came down in favour of 100 shares for the new FTSE Index.

The FT 30 Share Index over time
Figure 2.1 shows the course of the FT 30 Share Index over the years from its introduction in 1935. It shows behaviour that is typical of share price indices.

Typically, a period showing a general upward movement is followed by a subsequent fall in the general level of share prices, that is, bull market years are followed by bear market conditions. There are also fluctuations around these trends making it difficult to determine whether behaviour of the index in the last few weeks or months is to be interpreted as a change of trend or as simply a fluctuation around the continuing present trend.

The diagram also illustrates one of the major risks involved in investing in ordinary shares and holding them over a period of time. Inspection of the diagram shows that the purchase of a broad portfolio of shares corresponding to those that form the basis of the index would, if purchased just before the onset of a bear market, have meant significant capital losses over the next several years. also it is clear that such a purchase at other points' just before the onset of bull market years would have enjoyed substantial capital appreciation. Some of these points are marked on the diagram.

Whilst years of generally rising prices are followed by years of generally falling share values, there is no obvious regular time-related periodicity to the diagram. It is the irregularity of the graph that makes forecasting difficult if not impossible.

The new FTSE 100 Share Index

The Financial Times Stock Exchange 100 Share Index or 'Footsie' as it is known colloquially, formally came into existence in January 1984 to prepare the way for the new financial instruments that were introduced on 3 May 1984. It is a weighted arithmetic mean based index updated every minute and consequently has a number of advantages over the FT 30 Share Index.

Averaging the share price changes of 100 shares rather than 30 means that it is representative of a broader spread of shares. Certain groups of quoted shares are unrepresented in the 30 Share index but are included in the new index.

The arithmetic mean eliminates the 'downward bias' inherent in the geometric mean form of the 30 Share Index. Thus, the new index measures changes in the values of a portfolio invested in the 100 shares in the same ratios as the weights whereas this is not true of a portfolio equally distributed over the 30 shares of the FT 30 Share Index.

Publication of the latest updating of the index is intended to lag the conclusion of the relevant transactions by no more than a minute–a considerable improvement towards a 'real-time' index

Table 2.5 Example to show the method of calculation of the FISE 100 Share Index

Company	Capital (£m)	Weight	Price 4.5.1984	Price 5.5.1984	% price change	% price change × weight
1 Associated British Foods	19	0.013	172	170	−1.163	−0.015
2 Allied Lions PLC	167	0.115	174	170	−2.299	−0.264
3 Associated Dairies	70	0.048	184	184	0	− 0
4 BAT Industries PLC	91	0.062	248	245	−1.210	−0.075
5 British Home Stores	52	0.036	233	223	−4.292	−0.155
6 The British Petroleum Co. Ltd.	466	0.320	520	515	−0.962	−0.308
7 Barclays Bank PLC	282	0.194	488	490	+0.410	+0.080
8 Barratt Developments PLC	7	0.005	126	124	−1.587	−0.008
9 Bass Ltd	87	0.060	378	375	−0.794	−0.048
10 Beecham Group PLC	216	0.148	327	323	−1.223	−0.181
	1,457	1.001				−0.974

Notes: The weights do not sum to 1 due to rounding off to three decimal places. The average change in the general level of these share prices between the stated dates is a reduction of 0.974%

compared to the hourly intervals between updating of the FT 30 share Index.[16] Continuous updating is a necessary precondition for the introduction of certain financial futures contracts such as the FTSE 100 Share Index Futures Contract introduced on 3 May 1984. It ensures that all parties to making a market in these futures may be equally up-to-date with price trends and that traders at the centre of the action (on the Stock Exchange floor) do not have an unfair advantage over those somewhat further removed from actual share trading.

The index is in line with the construction of certain US counterparts such as the Standard and Poor's 500 index. The major reason for establishing yet another share price movement measuring formula was the introduction of stock index options and futures contracts in London similar to those that had been traded for some years already on the American stock exchanges.

Calculation of the FTSE 100 Share Index

Table 2.5 is illustrative but not fully detailed. The first ten of the companies in the new index in alphabetical order have been chosen to show how the index is calculated. The same weighting principle (market capitalisations) has been used but the numerical value of the weights will be different because only ten companies have been used, not the full complement of 100.

The largest single price change in the table is the reduction from 233p to 223p in the share price of British Home Stores–a reduction of 4.292%. Despite this, British Home Stores only contribute 0.155% to the overall price reduction of 0.974%. This is because we are using a weighted arithmetic mean. The capitalisation of BHS only represents 0.036 of the total capitalisation of the ten companies considered. Thus only 0.036 of the share price change is reckoned as the contribution of this price change to the average for the ten companies. In an unweighted arithmetic mean based calculation. 0.1 of the share price change or 0.429 would contribute to the overall change.

Capitalisations are only one possible basis for weighting the relative importance of the companies in the index. Sales or numbers of employees would provide a different but arguably reasonable set of weights.

It cannot be stressed often enough that there is no 'right' or 'wrong' method of calculating average price changes when constructing an index. Each form has its own inherent properties that makes it more or less suitable for a particular purpose.

From percentage change to index number

Average changes in stock market prices have been calculated using arithmetic and geometric forms of the mean. Such a calculation produces a percentage up or down in the general or average level of prices.

Changes in indices are not typically reported as having changed by a percentage–a particular index is said to rise or fall by a certain number of index points. A change of say 20 points in the FT 30 Share Index does not make sense unless we are told for example that it rose 20 points to its latest level of 1300. We then know that this was a rise in the average level of share prices of (20/1280) 100 = 1.56% A rise of 20 points that took the index to 500 would of course be a rise of 4.16%. Thus care is needed when statements are made in the media such as 'the Index fell today by the greatest number of points ever in a single day'. As should be clear from this paragraph, such a fall may well not be the greatest fall in one day in percentage terms. As an index increases in its numerical value, a given percentage change will be represented by a greater number of index points.

The FTSE 100 Share Index was introduced with a base of 1000. If, in the example in Table 2.5 the index stood at 1150 on 4 May 1984, then the fall of 0.974% would be recorded in index points as a reduction of 11.20 points (0.00974 × 1150) and the new index on 5 May 1984 would stand at 1138.80.

So far, we have had examples of important stock market indices based on the unweighted geometric mean and the weighted arithmetic mean. There is a very important example of the use of the unweighted arithmetic mean and it is to this that we now turn.

Dow Jones Industrial 30 Share Index

The present book covers statistical information relating to the British economy. The major world economies are becoming ever more interlocked and interdependent and statistics such as the Dow Jones Industrial 30 Share Index[17] are quoted alongside their British counterparts. Frequently now in the media, the Dow Jones 30 and

Table 2.6 The Dow Jones 30 Share Index – worked example

| | | New York Stock Exchange Closing Prices, 4.00 pm ($) | | | |
Company	21.1.1985	Movement	20.1.1985	% price change
1 Allied Corporation	32.250	0.625	31.625	1.9763
2 Aluminum Company	35.750	0.500	35.250	1.4184
3 American Brands	64.750	1.125	63.625	1.7682
4 American Can	50.375	0.500	49.875	1.0025
5 American Express	39.125	1.125	38.000	2.9605
6 American Telephone & Telegraph	21.125	0.625	20.500	3.0488
7 Bethleham Steel	19.625	0.750	18.875	3.9735
8 Chevron	32.625	1.500	31.125	4.8193
9 DuPont	49.375	1.375	48.000	2.8646
10 Eastman Kodak	72.125	1.625	70.500	2.3050
11 Exxon	48.125	1.500	46.625	3.2172
12 General Electric	63.375	2.875	60.500	4.7521
13 General Foods	55.125	0.125	55.000	0.2273
14 General Motors	37.375	−0.375	37.750	−0.9934
15 Goodyear	27.500	1.000	26.500	3.7736
16 Inco	13.750	0.875	12.875	6.7961
17 IBM	128.250	4.125	124.125	3.3233
18 International Harvester	10.000	−0.250	10.250	−2.4390
19 International Paper	54.625	1.875	52.750	3.5545
20 Merck	95.750	2.250	93.500	2.4064
21 Minnesota Mining & Mfg	84.000	2.750	81.250	3.3846
22 Owens-Illinois	39.625	0.875	38.750	2.2581
23 Proctor & Gamble	56.625	1.125	55.500	2.0270

24	Sears Robuck	35.000	1.625	33.375	4.8689
25	Texaco	35.000	1.000	34.000	2.9412
26	Union Carbide	39.250	0.375	38.875	0.9646
27	United Technologies	39.250	1.000	38.250	2.6144
28	US Steel	28.000	1.625	26.375	6.1611
29	Westinghouse Electric	29.250	1.375	27.875	4.9327
30	Woolworth	40.000	0.875	39.125	2.2364
		1,377.00		1,340.625	83.1442

the Financial Times 30 Share indices are broadcast together. For these reasons and because the Dow Jones Industrial 30 Share Index has some interesting computational characteristics that distinguish it mathematically from the indices so far considered, it is included in this book.

The Dow Jones Industrial 30 Share Index is one of four key indices published by Dow Jones & Co. Inc. in the United States.[18] it measures the average or central tendency change in the prices of those 30 shares chosen to be representative of American industry. arithmetically, it is an unweighted arithmetic mean with changing divisor and thus is rather different in construction to the FT 30 share and FTSE 100 Share indices considered so far. It dates in its present form from October 1928. Its distinguishing feature of a variable divisor to cope with the effects of 'stock-splits' is taken up in detail later.

The worked example in Table 2.6 covers the share price changes from close of business on the 'big board' of the New York Stock Exchange on 20 January 1985 to the close of business the next day, 21 January 1985. The *Wall Street Journal* European edition headlined this particular change-over 24 hours as 'Big Board Stocks Surge by 34.01 to 1261.37 for a One-Year High'.[19] This section looks at how these figures were arrived at and considers their economic and financial significance.

Calculations on the Dow Jones data

The following calculations are based on the data in Table 2.6:

	21 January 1985	20 January 1985
Total cost of a portfolio of the 30 shares in the table	$\dfrac{\$1,377.000}{1.132}$	$\dfrac{\$1,340.625}{1.132}$
Average cost per share of the portfolio using the reduced figure for the divisor (see text)	$ 1,216.431	$ 1,184.298

Change in the 'average' share price or the change in the total cost of the portfolio

$$= \ (\$1,216.431 - \$1,184.298)/\$1,184.298$$

$$= \quad (\$1,377.000 - \$340.625)/\$1,340.625$$
$$= \quad 2.71\%$$

Sum of the individual per-
centage price changes in the table
$$= \quad 83.1442$$
Average percentage increase
$$= \quad 83.1442/30$$
$$= \quad 2.771\%$$
Level of the index at the
close of business on 20 January 1985
$$= \quad 1,227.36$$
Increase as calculated above
$$= \quad 2.771\%$$
$$= \quad 0.02771 \times 1,227.36 \text{ index points}$$
$$= \quad 34.01 \text{ index points}$$
Level of the index at the close of business on
21 January 1985
$$= \quad 1,227.36 + 34.01$$
$$= \quad 1,261.37$$

Discussion of the calculations

The date on share prices such as that quoted for the two dates in January 1985 is available from several different sources. Convenient sources for UK readers are the *Wall Street Journal* European edition and the *Financial Times*. Price changes are recorded in multiples of $1/8 or 12.5c. Thus, all the prices move up or down in multiples of this fraction of the dollar. The data were decimalised for the table to facilitate subsequent calculations and therefore move in amounts of $0.125.

If all the 30 individual share prices for each date are added, a figure is obtained that is the cost of acquiring one each of the 30 shares. This amounts to the figure shown of $1,340.625 at the closing prices prevailing on the New York Stock Exchange on 20 January 1985 and $1,377.000 on 21 January 1985: an increase of 2.71%.

The sum of all the 30 individual percentage share price changes amounts to 83.1442%. Dividing by 30 yields the average percentage change of 2.771%. This is the calculation that leads to the figures headlined in the *Wall Street Journal* of Tuesday, 22 January 1985 and referred to above.

Between 1 October 1928 and the close of business on the New York Stock Exchange at 4.00 p.m. on 20 January 1985, the index had risen to 1,277.36. The further rise of 2.771% between then and the close of business the next day, 21 January, increased the level of the index by 34.01 points to the new headlined level of 1,261.37. (2.771% of 1,227.36 is 34.01).

Compare the 2.771% to the 2.71% of the previous paragraph. These figures are not derived from two different ways of calculating the same percentage figure. They have a different basis of calculation and are numerically quite different. They would only be numerically equal if all the initial individual share prices were equal. The following illustrative example will clarify this point.

Two shares in two different companies initially cost $1.00 each. Subsequently, one rises in price by 50%, the other by 25%. The new prices are thus $1.50 and $1.25. The average percentage price change is thus $(50 + 25)/2 = 37.5\%$. The average price per share also rises by 37.5%, from $(\$1 + \$1)/2 = \$1$ to $(\$1.50 + \$1.25)/2 = \$1.375$. In this case, the two percentages are equal.

Consider the same percentage changes in price from unequal initial prices of $1.00 and $0.90. The new prices are $1.50 (up 50%) and $1.125 (up 25%). The average percentage rise is again 37.5%. The average price per share rises from $(\$1.00 + \$0.90)/2 = \$0.95$ to $(\$1.50 + \$1.125)/2 = \$1.312$, a rise of 38.15%. The 38.15% and 37.5% in these illustrative examples differ for the same reason that the 2.771% and 2.71% mentioned in the paragraph above differ: namely, that the initial share prices on which the calculations are based are not numerically equal.

The divisor

The original divisor of this index back in 1928 was 30. After all, if one has 30 price changes, why divide by any other number than 30 if calculating an average price change? Why should the divisor have fallen from 30 in 1928 to 1.132 in January 1985 and further to 0.889 in January 1987?

Consider three shares initially priced at $1.50, $1.00 and $0.80. The average price is clearly the sum of these three prices divided by three – $1.10. Suppose the market now values the $1.50 share at

$1.00 because of a decline in the profitability of the company. The new average price is now $0.93, the divisor remaining three.

Suppose, however, that the same company had remained just as profitable as before but had made a bonus issue of shares, known as a stock-split in the United States and as a script issue in Britain, and that this amounted to one new share for every two existing shares held.[20],[21] The company's issued capital would have risen by 50% and the share price, because nothing else had changed, would have fallen by one-third from $1.50 to $1.00. Nothing real has happened to the company's fortunes, only a paper transaction has taken place. What about the divisor now?

Nothing has happened to change the market's valuation of the company but a single share now represents proportionally less of the company's value than before the stock-split. If this change happens in isolation from other changes, it may be argued that the average price of the shares should stay as it was before the stock-split. The average valuation of the three companies' real positions being the average share price, this should stay at $1.10. With individual share prices now $1.00, $1.00 and $0.80, this can only be achieved by reducing the divisor.[22] The new value of the divisor is thus x, where $2.80/x = 1.10$. Thus, the new divisor is 2.545.

Considerations of this nature explain the gradual fall in the divisor over 57 years of the life of the index from 30 to 1.132.

The average cost per share of the 30 shares that make up the Dow Jones Industrial Index, using New York Stock Exchange closing prices for 21 January 1985, was $1,216.431. This is derived using, for the reasons discussed above, a divisor of 1.132, not 30.

If we had divided by 30, the average price per share would have been $45.90. What claim does a price of $1,216.431 have to be more real a share price value than the straight averaging with a divisor of 30 to produce a figure of $45.90.?

The $45.90 contains a mixture of the real factors affecting share prices such as profitability, capital employed and growth actual and prospective, and the purely 'book-keeping' effects of all the stock-splits that have taken place over the years. The $1,216.431 is an average cleaned of the stock-split effects and reflects the impact of the changing real factors on the share prices of the index over the years. Just because something cannot be directly observed and must be calculated does not make it any the less real.

Thus, there are two types of average calculated for the Dow Jones indices. There is the calculation leading to the published changes in the indices themselves and the adjusted divisor calculations to produce the average share price. For the reasons discussed, these two values will normally be numerically different.

The divisors are published daily in the *Wall Street Journal* but not at the time of writing in the European edition of this newspaper.[23]

Historically, changes in the divisors may be traced in the Wall Street Journal Annual Index. For example, it is recorded that 'Starting with June 2's stock market prices, Dow Jones averages for the 30 industrial stocks . . . will give effect to General Electric's distribution of one additional share of common stock for each share held, to effect a 2 for 1 stock split; this changed the divisor for the thirty industrial stocks to 1.248.'[24]

Economic and financial significance of the index

Much of the comment earlier in the book about the significance of the FT 30 Share Index applies directly to the Dow Jones Industrial 30 Share Index. One may broadly think of the Dow Jones 30 Share Index as the American counterpart of the FT 30 Share Index in the United Kingdom. The mathematics of averaging are of course quite different: the Dow Jones 30 employs an unweighted arithmetic mean compared to the FT 30's unweighted geometric mean.

Both have been in existence so long as to become institutions in their own right and one should therefore be careful of reading too much into a given index change.

A rise or fall in the index requires an initial excess demand or supply in the stock market which then causes the price rise or fall to bring supply and demand again into equality. Therefore, the index will move to reflect changes in the buying and selling pressures in the market. An almost infinite number of possible combinations of factors may cause the index to change by a given number of points.

Broadly over the years of sustained economic growth, company profitability will tend to rise generally in line. This means that associated capital values and yields will also rise. Yields cannot rise too far 'out of line' with interest rates generally. Increasing yields will be 'brought into equilibrium' again in this situation by a share price rise as investors place their buying orders. Not only the actual but also the expected or anticipated yields will determine buying or selling decisions and thus price and index changes.

As index changes reflect actual or anticipated economic changes, the question arises as to whether indices of this nature systematically change in advance of indices of economic change or whether they follow as a reflector of prior changes elsewhere in the system. Research done in this area suggests that there is no clear relationship in time between such indices that is stable over time within one country or between countries. Thus, trying to use one to forecast the other is not likely to be a very fruitful exercise.

The other interesting question is the extent to which a series such as data on stock market prices contains information within the series that would enable one to forecast future values of the index on a basis other than that of pure guesswork. As already discussed elsewhere, the 'random-walk' hypothesis denies the view that many 'chart gazers' hold that these indices change in a systematic forecastable way.

As has already been mentioned there is another category of reasons why these indices are of interest: namely, the growing number of futures and other contracts already discussed that depend on index movements.

General investor concern with these indices is readily explained. Rising prices mean capital gains and losses with falling prices. As a summary, therefore, of what on average is happening price-wise, these indices are clearly of general investor interest.

Betting on an index

It has been possible for some years to bet on the direction and extent of the movement of a selected index over a given period of time. The example considered relates to betting on the FT 30 Share Index although there are similar wagers possible on dozens of commodity and financial indices in the United States and the United Kingdom. Several companies offer these facilities. What follows are examples to show the salient points involved when wagering on indices and is not a guide or description of what any particular company is offering as a facility at any particular point of time.

The gambler has first to decide which way the index will move, that is, 'up' or 'down' from its present level. This is the single most important decision to be made. Next, he must decide how much he wants to stake per index point moved over the period for which the bet is allowed to run. As gambling debts are binding in honour only and are not legally enforceable, he will also normally have to make a deposit of funds with the company offering the facility.

Illustrative example

Suppose the FT 30 Share Index on 1 April 1984 stood at 850. The gambler may be quoted two values of the related futures index, say 848 and 855 or the so-called buying and selling prices of the index. An 'up' bet would start at the higher price, 855, and a 'down' bet at the lower price 848. The spread between these 'prices' is the broker's spread and one of the major sources of income for the company offering the facility.

Consider now two alternative possibilities. Fourteen days later, the spread quoted is between 900 and 890. A successful 'up' bet would be terminated at the lower of the two values, that is, at 890. An unsuccessful 'down' bet would be terminated at 900. A successful 'up' bet would win (890–855) = 35 index points. An unsuccessful 'down' wager would lose (900–848) = 42 index points. The financial gains and losses are found by multiplying these points gains or losses by the amount staked per point moved: if £10 per point, the loss would be £420 and the gain £350.

Suppose the index had fallen over the 14 days and the quoted values of the index were 832 and 825. A successful 'down' bet would be terminated at the higher of these two values and an unsuccessful 'up' bet at the lower. A successful 'down' bet would thus win (848–832) = 16 index points and the unsuccessful 'up' bet would lose (855–825) = 30 index points. At £10 per point again, the winner would receive £160 and the loser would have lost £300.

Notice the asymmetry involved between winners and losers. For a given movement of the index, the unsuccessful wagerer loses more than the successful one. In a world where the direction of the index was purely random, this would always ensure that the company offering the facility received more from losers than it paid out to winners.

Uses of Stock Market indices

An index such as the FT 30 Share Index, the FTSE 100 Share Index or the Standard and Poor's 500 in the USA measures the average level of prices in relationship to an arbitrary base established in the past. Its rate of change up or down is a measurement of the rate of increase or decrease in the general level of share prices. A sustained upward movement is caused by more buyers than sellers at a given price and is commonly called a 'bull market'.

A sustained downward movement is caused by an excess of sellers over buyers at a given price and is known as a 'bear market'. The index thus acts as a summary indicator of the buying and selling activity over a period of time in terms of the levels of prices reached that this activity has generated.

There is a tendency to read a movement in the index as an indicator of what investors think is happening now and going to happen in the future in the economy generally. If a recovery from slump and depressed economic and financial conditions is likely, economic theory suggests that this may be preceded by a rise in the average level of stock market prices. Similarly, a downturn in the economy may be preceded by a sustained fall in stock market prices.

The reasoning is straightforward. A sustained rise in the FT 30 Share Index or FTSE 100 Share Index implies rising portfolio values and declining equity yields. The former effect will stimulate consumption expenditure in so far as this is a function of some measurement of wealth (including portfolio values) and the latter may stimulate investment as companies find it cheaper to make new issues of shares. The reverse is likely in the case of falling share prices.

If the above reasoning is correct and dominant enough to stand out against the welter of changes continuously occurring in the economic system, then significant correlations should exist between changes in stock market prices and some measurement of aggregate economic activity such as an industrial output index.

Considerable debate exists as to the precise nature and extent of any such causal links between stock prices and general economic conditions, although something of the process outlined above certainly seems to exist in a number of countries, particularly the United States. The strength and nature of the relationship appears to vary between countries.[25]

Advantages of a pure gamble

As the above example and many others of the same genre are regarded as gambling, the debts incurred are binding in honour only. Being regarded as gambling by the Inland Revenue, winnings

are free from all capital and income taxes although the corollary is
of course that no tax offset for losses is allowed.

The winnings are normally calculated as in the example above with
no deductions for commission or brokerage charges. Such charges
are incurred on buying or selling the other instruments available to
hedge views about the future course of share prices. Some of these
other hedging instruments are discussed below.

Stock Market futures

These are new developments that have come into existence over the
last two years or so, beginning in the United States with an index
future traded in Kansas in 1982 and making an appearance on the
London market from May 1984 based on the FTSE 100 Share
Index.

General background

Rising stock market prices and falling yields or falling prices and
rising yields mean rising or falling capital values of equity and gilt
portfolios. A portfolio manager is thus exposed to market risks of
variations in the values of the portfolios he manages. He may wish
to hedge or protect himself against these risks. The new futures
contracts provide a source to which he may turn in his search for
suitable hedging instruments.

Example of a futures contract

Such a contract was introduced by the London International
Financial Futures Exchange on 3 May 1984 and is based on the
FTSE 100 Share Index. With this contract, there is a fixed relationship between the FTSE 100 Share Index and the futures index
related to it. If the actual index stands at say 1170.5, then the
corresponding futures index stands at 117.05. The unit of trading,
the value of one contract, is then £25 × 1170.5 = £29,262.5.

Anyone contemplating such a contract must take a view about the
way he thinks the market will move before deciding whether to buy
or sell one of these contracts. If he correctly anticipates a rise in the
market, he will make a profit by buying a contract. If he correctly
forecasts a fall in the index, a profit will be made by selling a
contract.

Expecting the market to rise, a contract is bought at an index value of 107.00. A week later, the index has risen to 109.50. Expecting a levelling of or even a fall in stock market prices because of say an expected rise in interest rates, the contract is sold. The gain is 2.50 index points. This amounts to a gain of £250 per index point or £625 for the 2.50 points movements of the futures index. This is a very large amount requiring a 25 point movement in the FTSE 100 Share Index or approximately a 20% increase in the general level of share prices, given the level of the index at the time of writing.

Smaller movements create opportunities for profit and the reckoning is normally in 0.05 of an index point movement which corresponds to £12.50p or one 'tick' in the language of the market. There are 2.50/0.05 = 50 ticks in the above example. The gross gain before deduction of commission charges is thus again 50 × £12.50 = £625.

With the contract briefly discussed above, there is no certain loss knowable in advance. For the risk-averse, there may be advantage in an arrangement where a known maximum loss is built into the contract terms. Such an arrangement is a feature of another kind of contract, again introduced into London in May 1984.

Such a contract is the index option – a traded option on the FTSE 100 Share Index. One may buy a call option, that is the option but not the obligation to require the seller entirely at the buyer's option to sell to the buyer the index. The maximum loss to the buyer of such an option is then the premium or price paid to the seller, that is, the writer of the option. This is directly analogous to the purchase of a call option of the shares of a particular company, but is buying the index as a whole and not the equity of a particular company.

Worked example of an option contract on the FTSE 100 Share Index
Suppose a buyer has a 1075 call option but the index stands at 1145. The 70 index points difference is the so-called 'intrinsic value' of the contract and is the amount the buyer is entitled to receive by exercising his option from the writer. Each index point is worth £5 and thus the settlement in cash would be made by a cheque for £350 made payable to the exerciser of the option. The net gain for the buyer is then the £350 minus the premium paid for the acquisition of the option.

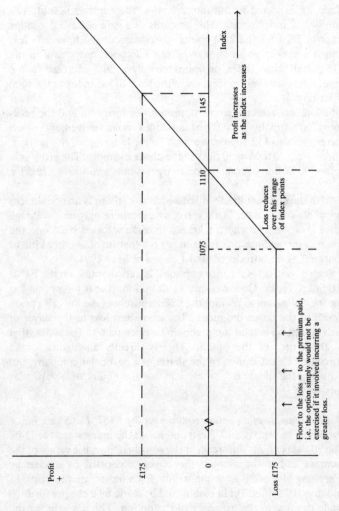

Figure 2.2 Characteristics of the call option discussed in the text

Profit +

£175

0

Loss £175

1075   1110   1145

Index

Profit increases as the index increases

Loss reduces over this range of index points

Floor to the loss = to the premium paid, i.e. the option simply would not be exercised if it involved incurring a greater loss.

The position of this option is illustrated in Figure 2.2. If the index stands at 1075, there is really no point in exercising the option. An exercise of a 1075 option at an index value of 1075 would involve a cheque for nothing, thus the loss would still be equal to the premium paid. Such an option may be worth exercising beyond 1075 because the cheque passed by writer to buyer in effect reduces the buyer's loss below the level of the premium paid. At an index of 1110, the cheque would equal 35 points × £5 = £175 which would enable the buyer to recoup his premium outlay. Beyond 1110, the buyer's profit and the writer's loss increase. For example, at an index value of 1145, the profit, if the option is exercised, for the buyer is £175, that is, 70 index points × £5 = £350 less the premium of £175. At this particular index value, the writer's loss is also £175: the payment of £350 minus the premium received of £175.

As is further discussed in Chapter 6 on traded share options, one of the main attractions of these contracts is not whether to exercise or not but rather whether the price of a given standardised contract will change by enough to make a profit by selling the option instead of deciding whether to exercise the option or not.

Notes

1 The Financial Times 30 Share Index introduced on 1 July 1935 averages the share price changes of 30 leading UK companies.
2 The Financial Times Stock Exchange 100 Share Index introduced in January 1984 averages the share price changes of 100 leading companies.
3 Continuous updating presents obvious problems. In periods of very busy trading there is the possibility that the posted value of the index may lag the values actually being recorded on the 'floor' of the Stock Exchange by an increasing amount.
4 There is a close connection between market capitalisation and shares outstanding. Shares outstanding = (market capitalisation)/(nominal share price).
5 Companies are changed from time to time in the FT 30 Share Index because of poor performance. At the time of writing, the most recent example of this was the replacement in November 1983 of Dunlop Holdings by Trusthouse Forte because Dunlop shares 'are no longer considered to be representative of the motor components industry'. See report in *Daily Telegraph*, 22 November 1983. For other changes since this time, see later in the chapter.

6   *Economist*, 20 July 1935, p. 135.

7   *Annual Abstracts of Statistics*, HMSO 1986. Recent base date changes include 16 January 1962 and 15 January 1974. The concept of a base date changes in detail later in the chapter.

8   W. S. Jevons, 'On the variation of prices and the value of the currency since 1782', *Journal of the Statistical Society*, May 1863, Vol. XXVIII, pp. 294–308.

9   Memorials of Alfred Marshall, p. 374 quoted in: L. Robbins, 'The place of Jevons in the history of economic thought', *The Manchester School*, Vol. VII, No. 1, 1936.

10 A. W. Flux, 'The measurement of price changes', *Journal of the Royal Statistical Society*, 1921, Vol. LXXXIV, pp. 167–215.

11 W. S. Jevons, *A Serious Fall in the Value of Gold Ascertained and its Social Effects Set Forth*, Edward Stanford, London, 1863.

12 The geometric mean of these two price changes is $2 \times \frac{1}{2} = 1$. Using 100 as the base year value of the index before the price changes, the index would remain unchanged after the price changes had taken place. The arithmetic mean of these two price change is of course $\frac{1}{2}(200 + 50) = 125$. Thus, the index rises by 25% from 100 to 125.

13 E. C. Rhodes, 'The precision of index numbers', *Journal of the Royal Statistical Society*, 1936, Vol. XCIX, p. 142.

14 'Instant updating for FT Ordinary Share Index', *Financial Times*, 8 July 1985, p. 1.

15 For a full discussion of the changes over the first 50 years of the index, see 'FT Ordinary Share Index: The First 50 Years', *Financial Times Survey*, 1 July 1985.

16 See comments on p. 31 concerning real-time basis of the FT 30 Share Index from July 1985.

17 Also known as the Dow Jones Industrial Average.

18 The other indices are a 20 share Transportation Index, a 15 share Utilities Index, and a 65 share Composite Index consisting of the 65 shares of the other three indices combined.

19 *Wall Street Journal*, Tuesday, 22 January 1985, European Edition, p. 17.

20 S. Stiegeler and G. Thomas, *A Dictionary of Economics and Commerce*, 1976, p. 37, Pan, for more details on bonus and script issues.

21 These bonus issues or stock-splits normally take place to bring down the individual share price to maintain investor interest. This is really a question of investor psychology. If he buys a £10 share or $2 \times £5$ shares after a split involving a doubling of the ordinary shares, he still acquires the same share in the equity of the company.

22 This assumes that the share price is the market's valuation of the 'real' position of the company.

23 *The Dow Jones Averages: A Non-Professionals Guide*, Educational Service Bureau, Dow Jones and Co. Inc., 1983.
24 *The Wall Street Journal Index*, 1983, p. 245.
25 For a survey of this particular relationship in a number of countries, see *Federal Reserve Bank of Kansas City Economic Review*, November 1983, Vol. 68. No. 9: 'Stock prices and industrial production in selected countries'.

Chapter Three

The Retail Prices Index

The annual rate of inflation, as measured by the 12-month change in the retail prices index increased to 5.7 per cent in December from the 5.5 per cent recorded in November.

Employment Gazette, January 1986, S5,
Department of Employment

Similar announcements are made in the media at monthly intervals to coincide with the latest updating of the index. This chapter looks at what such information means, at the construction and uses of the Retail Prices Index (RPI) and considers its limitations.[1,2]

Introduction

Economic analysis at all levels of sophistication makes use of such concepts as the General Level of Prices, the Rate of Inflation and the Cost of Living. Wage bargaining often includes a demand for compensation for any reduction in the real value of the wage due to inflation since the last 'wages round'. Distinctions between real and nominal magnitudes are increasingly made as inflation rates rise and such distinctions have always played a major role in the theorising of economists of every school. Such considerations permeate virtually the whole body of economic analysis and, therefore, we cannot avoid the problems inherent in attempting to measure the General Level of Prices and its rate of increase over time, or the Rate of Inflation. This chapter is devoted to a discussion of these measurement problems.

The final part of the chapter considers some of the uses to which the Retail Prices Index is put in the real world.

Some problems in the measurement of the Rate of Inflation and the General Level of Prices

The distinction between the General Level of Prices and the Rate of Inflation may be readily illustrated.

Assume that we are considering three commodities and that it is noted that, at a particular point in time, they are priced respectively at 2p, 3p and 7p each. The average price, using an unweighted arithmetic mean, is of course 4p. Suppose, one year later, it is observed that the prices are now 1p, 10p and 7p respectively. The average price is now 6p.

If these prices are converted into index form, the index rises from 100 to 150. The General Level of Prices is thus initially 100 rising to 150 one year later. The Rate of Inflation is then the rate of increase with respect to time of the General Level of Prices, that is, 50% in this highly simplified example.

The General Level of Prices may thus be thought of as the average of a particular set of individual prices at a particular point in time. One may think of the General Level of Prices in this example as rising from 4p to 6p. It is more generally the case that these figures would be represented by an index: thus, we interpret the above example as showing the General Level of Prices rising from 100 to 150.

The choice of 100 as the base figure to represent the General Level of Prices is arbitrary but has advantages which will become clearer as the chapter proceeds.

There are several measurement problems associated with the Rate of Inflation even if we confine our attention to one index such as the Retail Prices Index. Even accepting the data provided by government statisticians at its face value, there is still a problem. We can either measure inflation by averaging the 12 monthly values for each year in our series or by taking the December value for each year as a representative figure. Neither of these two alternatives is necessarily to be preferred to the other but the impression gained of inflation over a given period is affected by the method chosen. The choice of a particular series may be influenced by econometric consideration: if we have a model that expresses say the demand for money as a function of 'the' Rate of Inflation, we may care to choose the series that correlates most closely with variations in our dependent variable. But such statistical considerations apart, this fundamental problem of choice remains.

A more fundamental set of problems arises, however, when we consider that, in the United Kingdom with a population approaching 60 million people, there is no single index that can ever be totally relevant in its results to the environmental experiences of the population as a whole. We really need as many indices as people to reflect interpersonal differences in expenditure patterns. This is clearly not possible to achieve nor, even if it were possible, would it be desirable for we would lose the value of a summary statistic for the population as a whole. However, it is important to realise that we obtain the value of a summary statistic at the cost of its only indicating a central tendency and probably not being truly accurate for more than a small percentage of the population and strictly accurate for nobody.

Weights

The term 'weight' as used in the construction of the Retail Prices Index is probably the most common source of difficulty in

Table 3.1 Changes in the Cost of Living for one consumer related to varying percentages of his disposable income spent on a single commodity, related to price changes in that commodity

% income spent on good x	Price change in good X (%)	Change in Cost of Living of the consumer attributable to the price change in good X (%)	Inflation rate (%)
100	5	5	5
80	5	4	4
50	5	2.5	2.5
20	5	1	1
0	5	0	0

The change observed in this individual's cost of living is exactly equal to the rate of increase in the price of the one commodity when all his income is spent on it

understanding the construction, uses and limitations of the RPI, or of any other index for that matter.

Let us illustrate the meaning of the term by considering a situation where one person spends 100% of his disposable income on one commodity that remains homogeneous over time and is only on sale at one price at any given time whatever the geographical location of the points of sale. This is the simplest possible case in which to establish an index to measure inflation. It is likely to be the only situation in which a unique measurement of inflation is possible, but only for this one individual. Table 3.1 shows details of the index in such a situation.

As will be seen by inspection of the table, this equality breaks down as the percentage of disposable income spent on the commodity falls below 100%. Our first simple conclusion thus holds true only in the very special case of 100% of the individual's income being spent on one good. The equality between the change in price of one commodity and the inflation rate only holds in either these special highly unlikely circumstances or in the equally unlikely case of many commodities increasing equally in price. Consider a consumer spending 100% of his income on one good and earning the average weekly wage in 1982 of £191 per week for the top 10% of manual workers.[3] He would need a 5% increase in pay equal to £9.55 to maintain his real consumption levels or standard of living. If he were to spend only 50% of his disposable income on the good x, other things being equal, he would need an increase of 2.5% or £4.76 if he were on the average weekly wage mentioned above. The above discussion enables us to see the importance of the percentage of a person's budget that is spent on commodities undergoing price changes and how rates of increase in the cost of living or of maintaining a given standard of living relate to individual price changes. It also leads to the following equation:

Increase in the Cost of Living(%) resulting from a price change in a particular commodity X	=	increase in the price of X (%)	$\times$

The % of income spent on X (3.1)

In this equation, the percentage of income spent on good X is also known as the *statistical weight* applied to X. In other words, the contribution to changes in the cost of living made by price changes taking place in the markets for goods and services are estimated by *weighting* each price change by the percentage of income spent on each of the items in question. The weight can be regarded as a multiplier applied to the percentage individual price change to derive that item's contribution to the change taking place in the expenditure unit's cost of living.

An example to test understanding of equation (3.1)

Family A has an income of £30 per week after tax and family B an income of £50 p.w. likewise after tax. Family A spends 50% of its disposable income on food compared to 25% for family B. Food prices for both families rise by 50%. How much money do both these families require to just compensate for the increased cost of living?

Calculation for family A
Applying equation (3.1) the increase in the cost of living
$= 50\%(\frac{1}{2}) \times 50\%(\frac{1}{2}) = 25\%(\frac{1}{4})$
Therefore, the increase in income required $= 25\%(\frac{1}{4}) \times £30 = £7.50\text{p}$.
Thus, family A would require an extra £7.50 p.w. to compensate for the price change and to maintain its real consumption level and hence its standard of living. This does assume that other things are equal, that is, that no other price changes are taking place in the other items that make up this family's budget.

Calculation for family B
Again, as above, applying equation (3.1), the increase in the cost of living $= 50\%(\frac{1}{2}) \times 25\%(\frac{1}{4}) = 12.5\%(\frac{1}{8})$.
Therefore, the increase in income required $= 12.5\%(\frac{1}{8}) \times £50 = £6.25\text{p}$.
Thus, family B would require an extra £6.25p p.w. to compensate for the price change and to maintain its real standard of living. The rate of inflation for family B is half that of family A because it spends a smaller proportion of its income on the commodity increasing in price.

It is obvious from this example that a given price rise in one commodity will have radically different effects on the costs of living of individual units if there are substantial divergences in the percentages of their incomes spent on the particular commodity. In the real world, poor families spending large percentages of their smaller incomes on food will be disproportionately affected by food price increases compared to wealthier families spending smaller percentages of their larger incomes on the same items. It is the realisation of this that has led to a demand for the establishment of separate indices for particular groups such as pensioners and lower-paid workers.[4]

It is therefore necessary to weight items in the manner discussed above in order to make any statements about the impact of price changes on costs of living. This is true whether we are considering particular individuals or sub-aggregates such as 'all pensioners' or the 'low paid', or the population as a whole.

It is also clear that simply taking an arithmetic mean of all the prices of all commodities would be meaningless. To average say the price of oranges at five for 12p together with the price of apples at 20p per lb would be to produce a meaningless answer. A process of simply averaging a set of price increases only makes sense if all the prices refer to a single commodity, that is, if all the units averaged are homogeneous. The other situation which produces a meaningful statistical answer but which is unlikely to exist is shown in Table 3.2.

Table 3.2 Illustration that 'Weighting' is statistically not necessary in the unlikely event of all prices changing by the same percentage and in the same direction

Item	Weight (%)	Price change	Product (%)
A	10	5	0.5
B	30	5	1.5
C	20	5	1.0
D	15	5	0.75
E	25	5	1.25
Overall increase in the Cost of Living			5.00

Note: This yields the same result as an unweighted average of the individual price changes = $\frac{1}{5} (5 \times 5\%) = 5\%$

Here all the various commodities are weighted according to the percentages of consumers' incomes spent on each item, but all items have experienced the same price increase. In this unlikely case, the unweighted simple average yields the same numerical answer as the weighted result. This is not a likely situation in the real world.

Table 3.3 Calculation of the change in the Cost of Living for several items changing their individual prices by different percentages and directions

Item	Weight	Price change (%)	Effect on the Cost of Living %
A	10	5	0.5
B	30	20	6.0
C	20	0	0.0
D	15	−10	−1.5
E	25	20	5.0
Overall increase in the Cost of Living			10.0

The more general case is illustrated in Table 3.3. Here we have a situation where a number of different commodities are purchased. Over a given time period, differing percentages of income are spent on commodities undergoing price changes that are different as to both direction and extent. The effect of weighting is that we obtain a single combined estimate of these different price changes on the Cost of Living or the General Level of Prices of 10%, whereas a simple unweighted averaging would yield an answer of 7%. The reader who is still in doubt about the advantages of weighting price changes in this manner should work out, for any hypothetical initial income, the compensating increase in money income that leaves our individual just as well off after the price changes as before. 'Just as well off' means that he can buy just as much, no more but no less, after the price changes as before. He will find that a 7% increase in money income leaves our consumer undercompensated whereas the weighted result of a 10% increase in money income just maintains real income at the level prevailing before the price changes took place.

Alternative approach to 'weighting'

The layout of the official Retail Prices Index statistics differs from the presentation outlined above but conceptually amounts to essentially the same approach.

The sum of the weights in the official layout is 1000 with this figure divided among the ten summary classes of items in the index. An allocation of a weight of say 391 to food would simply mean that 391/1000 or 39.1% was the weight attached to food. This would have been derived from a sample of households and would be the representative figure for the group sampled. Two numerical approaches are possible. We can either proceed as above or as in Table 3.4. Let us assume a weight of 391 for 'food' and 609 for all other categories combined. This means that our survey data for the sample of households studied shows that £3.91 in every £10 is spent on food and £6.09 on all other goods. The layout of the calculation is then as in Table 3.4, assuming price increases of 10% for food and 20% for non-food (all other items).

Table 3.4 Calculation of the change in the Cost of Living, using weights expressed as parts of one thousand as in the Official Statistics

Item	Weight	Price change (%)	Product
Food	391	10	3910
other items	609	20	12,180
	1,000		16,180

Note: overall % increase in the Cost of Living = $\dfrac{\text{Sum of Product Column}}{\text{Sum of Weights}}$

$$= \frac{16,090}{1,000}$$

$$= 16.09$$

The weighted arithmetic mean increase in the Cost of Living, using the weight and price change data given above is thus 16.09%. This is clearly the same result as if we had proceeded as in our

previous examples. For comparison, that method is illustrated in
Table 3.5. It is important to realise that the two layouts amount to
the same thing as both layouts are fairly commonly met in the
literature.

Table 3.5 Calculation of the change in the Cost of Living using the
approach earlier in the chapter

Item	Weight	Price change (%)	Product
Food	39.1	10	3.91
Other items	60.9	20	12.18
Overall increase in the Cost of Living		16.09	

Continual sampling takes place to ensure that a representative
average value of a price change for each item is calculated.
Sampling locations are geographically spread to ensure representation of areas of differing purchasing power and population density.
Different types of retail outlets are also sampled to reflect the
sometimes wide range of prices that can prevail for a particular item
depending upon whether it is bought from say a supermarket or the
proverbial 'shop on the corner'.

The weights in the official index are obtained by studying the
budget patterns of a sample of households spread throughout the
United Kingdom. Households sampled are asked to keep a detailed
record of their expenditure pattern.

Omissions from the index

The index measures changes in the cost of buying a given basket of
commodities. Hence, it measures changes in the cost of maintaining
a given standard of living. It only does this perfectly for an
individual with expenditure patterns precisely in accord with the
offical weights. The more dissimilar price increases are and the
more 'deviant' is the expenditure pattern of an individual, the less
accurate is the index as a measure of changes in his cost of living.

Indeed, all of us spend on items not covered by the index. Income
tax payments, pension fund contributions, insurance premiums and

doctors' fees are omitted, because of problems of defining a 'unit' of such items. At a time when these items are increasing most rapidly and imposing most 'strain' on family incomes, failure to include them in the index is a major criticism of its coverage.

Absolute price levels and changes in the absolute level of prices

The tables show overall increases in the Cost of Living such that an income increase equal to this percentage would leave expenditure units with an income just maintained in real terms. These increases are also to be regarded as increases in the General Level of Prices. The absolute level of the General Level of Prices, as mentioned above, involves the concept of an index number base. The number 100 is usually chosen to denote the initial absolute value of the General Level of Prices at some base point of time. This value of 100 is arbitrary but does have some convenient advantages: it facilitates calculations in percentage terms but in theory could be any number. Let us assume that we have denoted the General Level of Prices as 100 at the beginning of the period to which the data of Table 3.3 applies. At the end of this period, the index will thus stand at 110. The numerical difference between 100 and the value of the index at any given time subsequently is therefore the percentage change in the General Level of Prices between the date of the establishment of the base of 100 and that given time.

The Retail Prices Index for the United Kingdom increased from 100 on 15 January 1974 to 349.7 on 10 April 1984. This means that the General Level of Prices, arbitrarily defined as 100 in January 1974 had risen to 349.7 by April 1984–an increase of 249.7% in the level.

The General Level of Prices and its rate of increase (the inflation rate) are therefore statistical constructs. The inflation rate measured by the Retail Prices Index is another example of the use of a weighted arithmetic mean. The arithmetic of the construction is identical in principle to that used in the calculation of the FTSE 100 Share Index reviewed earlier.

The frequency of base changes, namely 1956, 1962 and 1974, makes for problems in following changes in the General Level of Prices over a length of time but it is necessary to follow, albeit imperfectly, quality changes, the introduction of new commodities and the disappearance of old commodities no longer forming a significant part of consumer expenditure. It is of course possible to combine two or more indices numerically to form one continuous series.

The 'real world'

To establish an index, we have to allow for the problems discussed above but there are additional considerations. Official weights change over time. This partly reflects the fact that, as income changes take place, differing income elasticities of demand[5] ensure that variations take place in the percentages of income spent on the individual items in the index. The continual sampling of expenditure patterns enables the official weights to reflect these changes. This has to be done, otherwise the index would cease to measure changes in the Cost of Living, but it is bought at a cost. We cannot make very meaningful intertemporal comparisons in the Cost of Living owing to the .constantly changing weight composition of the index. Nor can we easily allow for quality changes in the nature of the commodities on sale. It should not be thought that the statistical methods used are defective; what one is trying to capture eludes summary in this way. Living standards consist of different quantities, qualities and types of goods at different points of time. Over long periods of time, these changes may well amount to trying to compare the costs of buying different quantities of goods that are completely different in nature. In such an extreme case, comparing the costs of two completely different bundles of goods may make easy comparisons of living standards virtually impossible by the use of an index.[6]

Uses of the Retail Prices Index

The Retail Prices Index measures the rate of increase in the average or General Level of Prices. It may thus be used to measure the decline over time in the value of or purchasing power of money.

If the Retail Prices Index doubles over a period of time, then it takes twice as much money to buy the same quantities of goods at the end as at the beginning of the period. The real value of a given unit of money will have halved.

Consider the Retail Prices Index, 100 at 15 January 1974, rising to 349.7 on 10 April 1984. This means that £1 on 15 January 1974 had the same purchasing power as £3.497 on 10 April 1984. Thus, £1 on the earlier date would have shrunk in purchasing power by the latter date to 1/3.497 = £0.29.

This is one example of the use of the Retail Prices Index as a deflator. As the word suggests, it deflates or reduces the value of money in line with the inflation experienced over a period of time.

An analogous procedure involving the use of an index as a 'deflator' may be used to convert money Gross National Product data into real Gross National Product data, that is, it is a way of correcting for price changes. Any differences in Gross National Product data remaining would then be attributed to output changes.

Comparisons with the Retail Prices Index are often made to demonstrate how well or badly certain other investments have performed over a past period of time. These are often read as a comment as to how well the particular investment had maintained its real value over time. Generally, if the market value of a particular investment has increased faster than the Retail Prices Index, its real value has risen. Real values fall if the asset has increased in price by less than the Retail Prices Index over the same period. Two examples of this use of the Retail Prices Index are now discussed.

Works of art

Investment in certain types of works of art is one way of trying to preserve the value of money. But how well have such investments done over a period of time? To assess this question quantitatively involves comparing two indices, the Retail Prices Index against an index of the values of works of art.

The Sotheby Index provides such an index. It is a weighted arithmetic mean of price changes for several categories of art. It is, therefore, similar in construction to the Retail Prices Index and the FTSE 100 Share Index. The Sotheby Index is set out in Table 3.6 for the period from December 1985 to December 1986. Ten major categories of works of art make a weighted contribution to a measurement of an average change in the value of this basket of items.[7]

The nature of the categories included in the index and the markets in which they are traded necessitates a different method of estimating weights and category price changes. The relevant

Table 3.6 The Sotheby Index

Item (1)	Weight (2)	Price change December 1985 to December 1986(%) (3)	Contribution to overall price change (%) (4)
1 Old master paintings	18	4.852	0.873
2 19th century European paintings	13	12.226	1.589
3 Impressionist paintings	19	28.953	5.501
4 Modern paintings	11	40.471	4.452
5 Continental ceramics	3	2.198	0.066
6 Chinese ceramics	11	8.186	0.900
7 English silver	5	12.245	0.612
8 Continental silver	5	11.207	0.560
9 French and Continental furniture	7	9.429	0.660
10 English furniture	8	23.464	1.877
	100		17.090

The procedure for calculating this index is identical to that involved in the arithmetic of other weighted arithmetic mean based indices. Each category of art in column (1) has a weight representing an assessment of its contribution to the overall price change. Each weight in column (2) is then multiplied by the price change for its category of art listed in column (3). The contribution of each category to the overall price change for the period is then recorded in column (4), and the sum of these individual contributions, 17.090% in our example, is then the weighted average price change for the categories listed in column (1) for the period December 1985 to December 1986.

information is collected from major sale rooms around the world and is then evaluated by experts.[8]

Collecting price information from the market, as in the case of the Retail Prices Index, requires that there is continuous trading of units as near homogeneous as possible. The nature of the art world is such that items sold are differentiated from other category items by various qualities such as style, date, and maker or painter, and that relevant sales take place infrequently. In these circumstances, the judgement of experts is substituted for the continuously generated market price data that is not available for these items.

Thus, from December 1985 to December 1986, the Sotheby Index rose by some 17% or, in index number terms, from 431 to 508. During the same period of time, the Retail Prices Index rose from 378.9 to 393.0, an increase of 3.72%.

In other words, over this period, works of art generally outperformed the Retail Prices Index. Thus, the real value of works of art generally rose as a consequence of their money values rising faster than the rate of inflation as measured by the Retail Prices Index.

Notice, however, the limitations of such statements. Comparing the Sotheby Index to the Retail Prices Index is asking the question how well did works of art generally perform compared to inflation over this period?

Inspection of Table 3.6 shows a wide range of percentage changes in the values of various categories included in the calculation. Modern paintings 'outperformed' the Retail Prices Index particularly well whereas Continental ceramics lost in real value over the period. Thus, it is not possible to use such an index to draw conclusions about changes in the value of a particular item that one may possess. The weights are unlikely to be those that would apply to an art portfolio possessed by any individual. Thus, the index would have to be used with very great care if one were trying to draw conclusions about the change in value of even a widely diversified art portfolio.

Arithmetically, one needs to clearly understand what may and what may not be compared. Percentages derived from index numbers may be directly compared. Thus, one may compare the 3.72% change in the Retail Prices Index to the 17% change in the Sotheby Index. Comparing the actual index numbers is useless unless they refer to the same base and date. The Sotheby Index has a base of 100 as at September 1975 whereas the Retail Prices Index

base date is January 1974, some 18 months earlier. For direct index
number comparisons to be made, it is also desirable that the
mathematical bases of the calculations should be the same. The
indices compared should all be arithmetic or geometric mean based,
not a mixture of both types.

Gold

An example is given in Table 3.7 of the direct comparison of two
indices with the same base dates. It shows clearly that, over the
decade from 1971 to 1981, gold outperformed the Retail Prices
Index, that is, gold rose in real value substantially over this period.

Table 3.7 Comparison of Gold Price Index with Retail Prices Index

Year	Retail Prices Index	Gold Price Index
1971	100	100
1972	107	140
1973	117	237
1974	136	407
1975	169	434
1976	197	416
1977	228	507
1978	247	604
1979	280	861
1980	330	1,582
1981	369	1,363

Source: The Kruggerand Directory 1971–1981 p.6

The series are directly comparable because they relate to the
same base date and have the same base value of 100. In this
example the series of index values for the Retail Prices Index would
have been altered from the official tables, as official base dates for
this index are January 1962 and January 1974. Such changes are
discussed below.

Table 3.7 shows a 269% increase in the Retail Prices Index
compared to a 1,263% increase in the price of gold. We are thus
invited to conclude that gold was an extremely good investment
over this period. Indeed, we can see that gold performed
spectacularly well over the period compared to inflation over the
period to 1981. What one should never do, however, is to simply

extrapolate trends such as those in the table to 1981 in order to forecast the period ahead. Such a divergence in the trends in two series is virtually certain to end at some time and perhaps go into reverse. To forecast the future on simple extrapolation is fraught with danger. What is needed is a properly specified model of gold price determination and one to determine the inflation rate. As such models exist but none are totally satisfactory, beware of attempting to use past behaviour to forecast the future unless you like a gamble with money you can afford to lose! At the end of April 1984, gold was priced at around $375 per ounce compared to $425 per oz on 1 July 1981, an 11.76% drop compared to a rise in the Retail Price Index between the same dates of some 17.70%, that is, an index increase from 297.1 to 349.7. By December 1986 the gold price was around $420 per oz whereas the Retail Prices Index had advanced to 393. The gold price at around the same level as at July 1981 had provided no protection against the 32.32% increase in prices over the same period.

The outstandingly good protection against inflation in the period covered by the table was followed by a period of years in which gold completely failed to provide protection against rising prices. The period after 1981 saw an increase in gold sales and a decreased demand for gold; both these factors make for a decrease in the price of the metal. There were Russian gold sales of some 90 tonnes in the 1980s to finance grain imports,[9] coupled to a decrease in demand for gold for the jewellery trade and other industries using gold as a raw material owing to the general world recession. Lower inflation rates generally in the industrialised world also meant a lower demand for gold as an inflation hedge.

It is also important to recognise that an index constructed on annual data may well distort what is actually taking place in the market by failing to reflect fluctuations that would be apparent if the index were constructed on say quarterly or monthly data.[10]

Cars
The *Practical Classics* car magazine publishes an old car index.[11] Compared to the Retail Prices Index, this shows how well or badly investment in classic cars generally affords protection against inflation. As inflation protectors over the period May 1980 to January 1983, old cars did not perform very well, showing only a

1.1% increase compared to 11.1% increase in the Retail Prices Index over the same period.

Notice that just as with all indices, this one is an overall market summary statistic. It is no specific indication as to the value of a particular car in a particular location just as the Retail Prices Index is no guide to the change in the price of a particular commodity.

Trade unions

A trade union may use the Retail Prices Index to argue the 'justice' of its particular wage or salary claim. This will often take the form of showing how far behind rises in the cost of living its members' wages have historically fallen. It may also use an index of earnings to argue that its members have fallen behind other groups of workers.

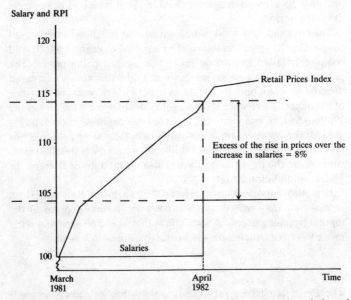

Source: adapted from *Salaries-Cash Limits or Negotiations* Association of University Teachers, 1982, p.2

Figure 3.1 Comparison between university teachers' salaries and the Retail Prices Index

The use of indices in this way is illustrated by an extract from a publication of the Association of University Teachers.[12] The union argued that 'no sooner had we "caught up" than we were forced behind once again'.[13] The general argument applies not only to wage and salary negotiations but to any situation where inflation is a continuous process but where payments to particular groups, whether wages or pensions, are readjusted periodically and retrospectively with respect to inflation.

Figure 3.1 shows the continuous nature of inflation compared to the periodic adjustment of salaries. The pay award of 5% in April 1982 represented a partial 'catching up' with prices but still a fall in real incomes. To maintain real incomes, a 13% rise would have been required. The diagram then shows further erosion of real incomes after April 1982.

There have been a few months when the RPI has actually fallen. For example, the Retail Prices Index fell from 323.1 in August 1982 to 322.9 in September 1982 and from 326.1 in November 1982 to 325.5 in December 1982.[14] These falls are insufficiently large and occur on too few occasions to constitute a major qualification to the above argument.

Pensions

Consider next a situation where there is 'full indexing' as in the case at present in the United Kingdom in relationship to index-linked pensions such as the Retirement Pension and certain public-sector occupational pensions such as that of schoolteachers. This is summarised in Figure 3.2.

In this example, the pension is fully indexed, that is, the real value is restored at discrete points of time, one year apart. If over one year, 20% inflation is experienced, a 20% increase in the pension fully restores the purchasing power so that the purchasing powers of the pension are equal at times t and $t1$. This does not restore the progressively reduced purchasing power over the period between pension adjustments. To achieve that at $t1$ would require a pension increase equal to the shaded area in the diagram.

In practice, of course, it is not possible to increase a pension by the amount of the inflation up to the date on which the increase takes place. For administrative and organisational reasons, the inflation adjustment will relate to inflation up to a point some time before the adjustment takes place. In the case of the Retirement

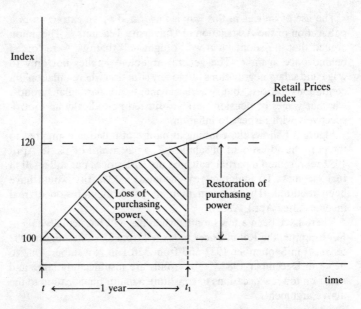

Figure 3.2 Comparison of fully indexed pension and the Retail Prices Index

Pension this is increased 'in line with inflation' in November each year but to inflation calculated up to the previous May. The 'pension year' runs from November to November whereas the 'inflation year' runs from May to May, creating a problem analogous to that discussed when considering the index-linking of gilt-edged securities. If the inflation rate is rising over time, it will be higher in the period May to November than in the previous period November to May: thus, the indexed adjustment will fall short of restoring the pension to the line tracked by the Retail Prices Index in Figure 3.2. If inflation is falling, then the adjustment may take the percentage increase in the adjusted pension above the line.

Building Societies
Indexing arises because of the non-neutrality of money during

Table 3.8 Building society interest on deposits and the Rate of Inflation

	1972	1973	1974	1975	1976	1977	1978	1979	1980	1981	1982
Building society interest on deposits	4.61	6.04	6.88	6.74	6.61	6.13	5.65	7.67	9.77	8.71	9.12
Retail Prices Index	7.11	9.19	16.05	24.24	16.54	15.85	8.30	13.39	17.97	11.87	8.60

Source: Annual Abstract of Statistics, HMSO, 1982, Tables 18.6 and 17.13

periods in which the General Level of Prices is either rising or falling. During periods of inflation, the monetary system favours certain groups in society and works against the interests of others–it is not neutral between them.

For example, borrowers from building societies benefit from the reduction in the real value of their debt whereas lenders to building societies lose, especially if the net after-tax rate on deposit accounts is less than the rate of inflation. Inflation thus effectively transfers real resources from the lenders to the borrowers as there is no mechanism, in the absence of the index-linking of mortgage debts, to enable lenders to participate in the increased nominal values of the properties financed by their lending. To achieve equity in this area would involve index-linking of mortgage debt. The obvious political difficulties are likely to preclude any such moves in this area.

A comparison of the Retail Prices Index to the after-tax yield on building society deposit accounts is one way of measuring the extent of this non-neutrality of money. Inspection of Table 3.8 shows that in 1982, for the first time in a decade, the inflation rate was actually lower than the after-tax return on a building society deposit account. Thus, for the first time, depositors experienced a rise in the real value of money held on deposit.

The Retail Prices Index is subdivided into a number of sections. For certain purposes, a subsection of the index may be more relevant than the overall or 'All Items Index'.

An insurance company may wish to insist on sums insured rising in line with prices. The householder may wish to know that he is 'adequately covered' against loss or damage to his household contents. The most appropriate measurement of inflation for this purpose is not the overall Retail Prices Index but rather the section 'Durable Household Goods'. This may rise at a higher or lower rate than the overall index. An insurance company may explicitly require its policyholders to index-link their cover to this section of the index.

The Cooperative Insurance Society states that 'your sum insured is index-linked and automatically moves monthly in line with the percentage change in the Durable Household Goods Section of the Retail Prices Index'.[15]

Indices for vulnerable groups

Problems may arise when measuring changes in the cost of living of certain groups in society such as the aged and the employed but low paid groups of workers.

Two major problems arise. First, expenditure patterns of such groups may differ significantly–their distribution of expenditure may imply different weights from those derived from a sample of households across a broad spectrum of middle-range incomes. Secondly, they may be limited to a narrower choice of retail outlets in which to shop. Owing to a lack of personal transport, they may be restricted to purely local shops and pay significantly more for each item than those whose means allows them to 'shop around'.[16]

There are three indices published regularly that attempt to reflect the different expenditure patterns of these groups. The government itself surveys one and two-pensioner households and the Low Paid Price Index does the same for the lowest paid 10% of households in the U.K. The latter is produced jointly by the Civil and Public Servants Association and the Low Pay Unit.

Pensioner indices

The introduction of special indices for pensioners was recommended in 1968. Death unfortunately means that a significant proportion of pensioners live in single-person households. The report led to the introduction of two indices, one for single-pensioner households and one for two-person households.

Table 3.9 shows the difference in weights for pensioner and non-pensioner households. It reflects what one would imagine but was based on the results of surveys into the budgetary expenditure of such groups. Although based on surveys, the weights are in the direction that a little consideration would suggest. The pensioners spend a higher proportion of their generally, but not always, lower incomes on fuel and light. Presumably, they spend more time at home during the day than those working, and this accounts in part for the differences. One would expect this group to spend a higher proportion of their incomes on food, again given the fact of generally lower incomes.

The government is convinced that the Retail Prices Index does not give significantly different results compared to the pensioner indices. The government argued in 1977 that 'the lack of major

Table 3.9 Weights for pensioners and non-pensioner indices

Item	One-person pensioner index	Two-person pensioner index	Retail Prices Index
Food	380	387	236
Alcoholic drink	26	49	88
Tobacco	31	52	42
Fuel and light	206	146	77
Durable Household goods	41	43	81
Clothing and footwear	64	60	82
Transport and vehicles	31	79	186
Miscellaneous, e.g. books and travel	90	85	89
Services, e.g. postage, telephone, TV licence, laundering, dry-cleaning	113	85	77
Meals outside the home	18	14	42

Note: As the weights sum to 1000, divide by 10 to express them as
percentages of income spent on the various categories of expenditure
Source: *Department of Employment Gazette*, May 1984, pp. 235–6, April
1984, pp. 104–5

Table 3.10 Comparison between pensioner index and RPI

Year	One-person pensioner household index	Retail Prices index	% difference
1974	114.2	116.1	+1.66
1975	145.0	145.7	+0.48
1976	171.3	168.0	−1.93
1977	194.2	190.8	−1.75
1978	207.1	205.3	−0.87
1979	239.8	239.8	0.00
1980	275.0	271.8	−1.16
1981	304.5	300.5	−1.33
1982	327.4	320.2	−2.20
1983	342.3	335.4	−2.02

Source: *Department of Employment Gazette.* October 1977, p. 977

differences between the overall rise in the general and pensioner indices is a sign of the strength and reliability of the general index as a measure of the impact of price changes over a broad range of households'.

Study table 3.10 and draw your own conclusions as to any significant differences between the indices. Inspection of the percentage differences in the table between the one-person pensioner household index and the Retail Prices Index shows that the latter does systematically underestimate changes in the cost of living of one-person pensioner households compared to the pensioner index itself. As the index-linking of pensioners is to the Retail Prices index, this is an added burden, albeit perhaps small numerically, in addition to the other problem of indexing pensions discussed above.

It is left to the reader to decide how significant the numerical differences between the two indices are for the welfare of pensioners.

Low Paid Price Index

The Low Paid Price Index was introduced by the Civil and Public Servants Association and the Low Pay Unit on 1 June 1978. It is based on the expenditure patterns of the lowest decile of wage-earners, that is, the poorest 10%.

One would make similar observations in relation to an index for the low paid as one would for pensioners. The relatively low incomes of both groups mean that the weights in the Retail Prices index are likely to be inaccurate and both are not as likely as the broad mass of middle-income groups to face the same price opportunities.

A given price increase contributes to the overall change in an individual's cost of living in direct proportion to the weight attached to the item. An example of this is shown in Table 3.9.

The weights used in the Low Paid Price Index are derived from the same source as those for the Retail Prices Index, namely, the annual Family Expenditure Survey.[17] As these are weights derived from the expenditure patterns of the lowest decile (the poorest 10% of working households), they tend to follow a pattern in relationship to the weights for the Retail Prices Index. These poorer households spend characteristically more on food as a proportion of their incomes as well as on fuel and light and housing. They tend to spend less as a proportion on such expenditure as durable household goods, clothing, and transport and vehicles.

The effect of these characteristically different weights is that their cost of living will be increasing faster than that of the broad mass of people if food and fuel and light prices are increasing more rapidly than for other categories.

The consequences for the measurement of changes in the cost of living of this group of using an index with weights that represent their expenditure patterns compared to the Retail Prices Index is illustrated in Table 3.11.

Table 3.11 Changes over 12 months in the Low Paid Price Index compared to the Retail Prices Index

Date	Low Paid Price Index (%)	Retail Prices Index (%)
March 1983	6.1	4.7
April	4.3	4.0
May	3.7	3.4
June	3.8	3.7
July	4.3	4.1
August	4.9	4.9
September	5.4	5.4
October	5.3	5.2
November	5.2	5.2
December	5.4	5.6
January	5.1	5.4
February	5.3	5.5
March	5.5	5.7

Source: CPSA Low Pay Unit, May 1984

Although the percentage difference between the two indices are fairly small, they assume a greater significance in that they relate to measurements of changes in the cost of living of the poorest 10% of wage-earners.

Notes

1 Monthly updating of the Retail Prices Index is to be found in the *Employment Gazette* published by the Department of employment.
2 E. E. Rowley, 'The Retail Price Index', *Economics*, Vol. XV, Pt. 3, No. 67, Autumn 1979, pp. 80–4.
3 Table 6.21, *Annual Abstract of Statistics 1984*, HMSO.
4 See pp. 75–8.
5 This term is used by economists to refer to the percentage change in expenditure on items as income changes. Such responsiveness or elasticity will of course vary from individual to individual at a given level of income and also vary as incomes vary.
6 An exercise to develop an understanding of these points may be found in: E. E. Rowley, 'The Retail Price Index', *Economics*, Vol. XV, Pt. 3, No. 67, Autumn 1979, pp. 80–4.
7 The example is of the ten-category index measured in sterling. There is also a twelve-category index published in the United States and measured in dollars. This includes the additional categories of American paintings and American furniture. There can be no simple relationship between the two indices. This is partly because of the different coverage of the two indices but mainly because of the ever changing exchange rate between the dollar and sterling.
8 From information kindly supplied by Jeremy Eckstein, Research Manager, Sotheby Parke Bernet & Co.
9 *Economist*, 4 July 1981, p. 82.
10 See p. 34 for comments on the reasons for introducing the FTSE 100 Share index alongside the FT 30 Share Index.
11 Lindsay Porter, 'Market Trends', *Practical Classics*, January 1983.
12 *Salaries – Cash Limits or Negotiations?*, Association of University Teachers, 1982.
13 ibid, p. 3.
14 See monthly Retail Prices Index data in *Department of Employment Gazette*.
15 On annual invitation to renew policies.
16 *Report of the Cost of Living Advisory committee*, Cmnd 3677, HMSO, 17 May 1968.
17 The Family Expenditure Survey was introduced in 1957. It samples some 11,000 addresses with a response rate of about 70%. Its main purpose is to provide information for the weighting pattern of the Retail Price Index. See *Annual Abstract of Statistics 1984 edition*, HMSO, p. 261.

Chapter Four

The European Currency Unit

Why an international currency?

It is England that should have suggested free trade in money to the world; it is Manchester that should have suggested it to England . . . It is a new step in the rapprochement of nations and the spread of civilisation . . . we have lost the opportunity of initiating this great reform . . . if we refuse to accept it when offered by a foreign government . . . we shall stultify ourselves and act unworthily of [the] position which we occupy in the commerce . . . of the world.

William Stanley Jevons, 1868[1]

The idea of an international currency is thus not new. It was advocated by the Manchester economist W. S. Jevons in 1869. The extract above could have been written now by an economist or politician advocating Britain's full membership of the European Monetary System.

Some of the advantages mentioned by Jevons in his 1868 paper still hold good over a century later. It would, he argued, be of convenience to travellers to be able to pass the same money in whatever country they may visit. The same point was made in 1982 in a question by a member of the European Parliament to the European Commission as to 'when does the Commission intend to introduce an ECU [European Currency Unit] bank note in a single value in relation to the currency of each member State'.[2]

The same member of the European Parliament, Dieter Rogalla of Denmark, had earlier pointed to a problem that all-night service pumps in Holland operated only on Dutch banknotes and that ECU notes might be advantageously introduced to minimise payment difficulties for fuel on major European motorways at night.[3] Presumable such ECU notes, if introduced, would circulate alongside units of the national currency in much the same way as Bank of Scotland notes in England at the present time.

Problems exist that were not present in Jevons's day. Coins and notes are not now simple multiples or fractions of each other in the various member states of the EEC. Such relationships that do exist alter, both due to day-to-day fluctuations in exchange rates and changes from time to time in central rates of exchange between the currencies. The punt, the national currency of the Republic of Ireland, circulated at one time in parts of the United Kingdom because of the parity maintained between it and the pound sterling. The breakdown of that parity and the associated fall in value of the punt in relation to the pound sterling caused the former to be no longer so acceptable, that is, individuals could no longer be certain of a known simple relationship of value to the pound sterling. This is precisely the problem of fluctuating exchange rates that would make it extremely difficult to introduce and maintain in circulation throughout the member states any ECU note or coin.

It is thus not possible, under present arrangements, to define an ECU note that would have a ready counterpart in an already existing national state coin or note. Europe in the 1860s was bound by the exchange rate linkages of the gold standard and counterpart coins in terms of gold content in each country. It is through the creation of the European Monetary System that Europe, in seeking to create 'a zone of monetary stability',[4] is trying to re-establish some of these characteristics of the monetary integration and stability of the late nineteenth century that disappeared with the Great War of 1914–18 and its consequences.

The second advantage of an international currency, in Jevons's view, was that conversion from one currency to another would be facilitated especially when 'we have a decimal currency of our own unit of value'.[1] The point is obvious enough that conversion arithmetic is easier if notes and coins are simple multiples of subdivisions of each other but modern calculators reduce the importance of this point for the present day.

The overwhelming advantage for Jevons in having an international currency lay in the extension and promotion of free trade–always at risk in a world of national currencies and exchange rates. The unification of currencies was seen as the appropriate sequel to the introduction of free trade and a necessary move to preserve it.[1]

Establishing and maintaining multilateral trade are certainly aims of the European Economic Community. Article 110 of the Treaty of Rome that established the EEC on 25 March 1957 provides for 'a customs union . . . to contribute to the harmonious development of world trade, the progressive abolition of restrictions on international trade and the lowering of customs barriers'.

Countries often resort to restrictions on trade in order to remedy balance of payments problems. Such problems arise for a number of reasons but inflation rate differences are a major cause. Such differences are often caused by uncoordinated rates of expansion of national currencies. The adoption of a single currency would prevent this happening and thus facilitate unhindered trade flows.

It would in effect link countries together like regions of one country and promote a federal union. National sovereignty and freedom to determine one's own monetary policies would cease. In all probability, one central bank would replace the central banks of the member states. It is precisely for these reasons that many people would oppose the introduction of an international unit as a comprehensive replacement for their own national currencies.

The ECU

The original *écu* was created between 1266 and 1270.[5] It was a gold coin, so called because it had a shield or *écu* on the reverse side.

The European Currency Unit (ECU) is the unit of account of the European Economic Community. Any such grouping of nations has a problem deciding upon a common unit of account in which community transactions shall be valued. The use of any one national currency is certain to be resisted by the other member states and each will probably wish its own national currency to be represented in the unit chosen. This leads naturally to the idea of a community unit of account consisting of a 'basket' of the national currencies of the member states.

Composition of the ECU
How much should each national currency contribute to the basket? This resolves into the question of choosing appropriate weights–analogous to the discussion of weighting problems considered in relationship to some of the indices in other chapters.

It seems not an unreasonable proposition that the amounts of the various currencies in the basket should reflect the relative importance of the economies of the member states. Intuitively, one would expect say the German mark to figure more significantly in the unit than the Greek drachma. But how should a quantitative assessment of the weights to attach to the various currencies be made? What is an appropriate measurement of the relative strengths of the economies of the member states of the EEC?

Introduction of the ECU

To obtain weights for the ECU, percentage shares in the total Gross National Product of the Community averaged over the five years from 1969 to 1974 were taken together with average shares over the same period in European destination exports of goods and services. Thus, the 17.5% weight for sterling meant that the United Kingdom's share in Community output and trade as defined above was 0.175 of the total for the Community as a whole for the period relevant to the calculation.

The original unit of account of the EEC was the European Unit of Account introduced on 28 June 1974, becoming the European Currency Unit in 1979. These units were both equal to 45.8564 Belgian francs. An odd amount you may well think!

It just so happened that this odd amount of Belgian francs was equal to $1.20635 on 28 June 1974, which was, in its turn, equal in value on the same date to one Special Drawing Right Unit, the unit of account of the International Monetary Fund. Thus, by setting the new European unit equal initially to the value of the other major international unit, continuity was maintained.

The individual national currency amount in the basket

The sterling weight, as explained above, was 0.175. Thus, the Belgian francs equivalent of sterling's contribution to the basket was the sterling weight multiplied by the total value of the unit in Belgian francs: $\cdot 175 \times 45\cdot 8564 = 8\cdot 02487$ BF. Multiplying this by the then exchange rate between sterling and the Belgian franc produced the sterling contribution to the basket of £0.0885. Repeating this calculation for the other eight member states at that time produced the basket composition shown in Table 4.1.

The results of the pressures that build up over time are shown in

Table 4.1 The ECU

Currency	Original basket from 1.1.1979	% of basket 1.1.1979	% of basket 12.7.1984	Revised basket from 17.9.1984	Weight in revised basket (%)
German mark	0.828 DM	27.3	37.2	0.719 DM	32
Dutch guilder	0.286 DG	9.0	11.4	0.256 DG	10.1
Pound sterling	£0.0885	17.5	14.7	£0.0878	15.0
Belgian and Luxembourg franc	3.80 BF	8.2	8.4	3.85 BF	8.5
Danish krone	0.217 DK	3.0	2.7	0.219 DK	2.7
French franc	1.15 FF	19.5	16.8	1.31 FF	19.0
Irish punt	0.0076 IP	1.5	1.0	0.00871 IP	1.2
Italian lira	109 L	14.0	7.9	140 L	10.2
Greek drachma	–	–	–	1.15 GD	1.3

the table. The 'strong' currencies of Europe increase their percentage shares of the 'basket' over time. This is illustrated most vividly by the German mark appreciating from 1979 to 1984 by some 36%, that is, from 27.3% of the basket to 37.2%. The 'weak' currencies, illustrated strongly here by the Italian lira, decrease their percentage shares of the basket. These changing percentage shares occur because of appreciating or depreciating national currency exchange rates in terms of other currencies. One of the most significant explanatory variables for this is the range of inflation rates experienced in the member states. The low inflation rate in Germany is the main reason for the appreciation of the mark as the relatively high inflation rate in Italy is for the depreciation of the percentage share of the lira in the ECU basket.

If these pressures were allowed to continue, without response, the basket would become progressively more dominated by the 'strong' currencies. One or two national currencies, principally led by the mark, would become the unit of account of the EEC. To remedy a situation like this, there is provision for periodic review of the basket. 'Strong' currencies tend to be reduced in the basket and the representation of 'weak' currencies increased so that overall, the contents of the basket in terms of national currencies are such that the relative contributions to EEC output and trade are reflected in the composition of the basket'. Examination of the revision of the basket in the table shows the response discussed here.

Value of the ECU in national currencies

The values of the ECU in a number of national currencies, both within and without the ECU basket, are published by the European Commission and by the financial media. This is quite easy to do as long as there is an exchange rate between the national currency in question and each of the components of the ECU. For example, if we wish to know the value of the ECU in terms of the Finnish markka, then the exchange rate between the markka and the currencies listed as the components of the ECU in Table 4.1 for the September 1984 revised unit are used to value these individual components. The sum of the values of the components in terms of the Finnish currency is then the value of the ECU in terms of the markka.

The United Kingdom and the European Monetary System

The United Kingdom is not, at the time of writing, a full member of the European Monetary System. The UK is represented in the ECU but does not accept the obligation to maintain sterling to within the ±2.25% limits that is necessary for full membership. There are a number of reasons expressed for adopting this position.

On the political level, there is opposition from those who would wish to see the United Kingdom distance itself from any particular scheme that looks as if it means a sacrifice of political independence and possibly a step towards even closer European unity.

The United Kingdom, alone of the member states, is an oil-producing country. It is, therefore, argued that sterling is likely to move upwards in value due to an oil price increase just as the same factor is causing the currencies of the other member states to move in the opposite direction. It is argued that this would make it especially difficult for the UK to hold to an agreed set of central rates.

The UK has a relatively very open economy. The significance of this is that many of the strongest forces determining exchange rates are generated outside the UK. This would, opponents of full membership argue, mean that the UK would have considerable difficulty in maintaining agreed parities.

The UK, together with Italy, has experienced some of the highest inflation rates of the member states. This means that the pound sterling would tend to be under pressure and present difficulty for the monetary authorities to hold its exchange value to within the agreed range around the central rate. This point has lost a lot of its earlier force as inflation rates in the UK have fallen considerably in recent years.[6]

Despite these arguments, at least one committee has recently strongly advocated that the UK should fully join the European Monetary System.[7]

The economic arguments for a fixed exchange rate system stem principally from a desire for stability and to avoid the use of the exchange rate as an instrument of 'beggar-my-neighbour' policies. Such policies might involve the use of devaluation to promote one's own exports at the expense of those of a trading partner–in effect, exporting unemployment and being threatened in due course with retaliation. More stable exchange rates also aid trade by reducing the costs of providing forward cover[8] and simplifying costing and pricing decisions.

Not every economist and politician is convinced of the desirability of a fixed rate system. The decision to base European monetary union on a grid of fixed exchange rates has been described as a 'return to the pain and frustration of a fixed rate world'.[9]

A fixed exchange rate between the currency of a country with a recurring tendency to a balance of payments surplus and one with a tendency towards a deficit means inflation for the surplus country and unemployment for the deficit trading partnet. In recognition of the problem of maintaining fixed rates over a period of time, the Treaty of Rome that established the EEC provides for close cooperation and coordination of the monetary policies of the member states.[10] One institutional expression of this cooperation is the Monetary Committee of the Economic Commission. Its membership consists of senior personnel from the treasuries and central banks of the member states. Part of its activities includes the preparation of reports on problems of national policy harmonisation.

The future of the ECU

Official uses of the ECU are not in doubt. The unit will remain as the unit of account of the EEC for official purposes. There are, however, substantial problems to be overcome if the unit is to become more widely used by the private sector.

There is a marked preference for invoicing in the traders' own currencies or those of their customers. This is what has been described as a 'preferred monetary habitat'.[11] The relative strengths of exporters and importers then determines which currency shall be used for any particular foreign trade transaction.

Why should a company prefer to hold a composite unit such as the ECU? If it operates in a number of foreign markets, it may well prefer to hold foreign currency denominated bank accounts in proportion to its business in the respective markets, in effect, to determine its own currency basket. The abolition of exchange controls in the UK in 1979 has made these operations considerably easier.

If the world returns to a period of violently fluctuating exchange rates, there may be a preference to move into those currencies appreciating in value rather than to hold a composite unit that 'irons out' fluctuations in value of the constituent currencies.

Making payments to or receiving moneys from EEC organisations using the ECU as the unit of account may indicate the desirability of holding an ECU denominated account.[12] It is not at all clear why this should be so because it would be a simple procedure to convert such receipts into a preferred single national currency or to reverse the procedure in the case of having to make ECU payments to an EEC organisation.

Some of the necessary conditions for more widespread use of the ECU are developing. A major problem is to find a market for the onward lending of received ECU denominated deposits which, in its turn, would generate receipt of ECU deposits by other banks. Such a flow around the system would encourage further more widespread use of such accounts. Such a relatively free flow of deposits around the system is contingent upon the development of a clearing arrangement. The establishment of such a scheme is currently under active development.[13]

Commercially the ECU is a cumbersome unit. To establish deposit rates, for example, the unit has to be split into its constituent currencies and a weighted average of the interest rates on these calculated. This is fairly time-consuming. In summary of the above, the ECU is far from operating as a parallel currency, let alone anything remotely resembling a replacement for the individual national currencies. Only time will tell which way the ECU will go.

Some uses of the ECU

A company will have no alternative but to consider the ECU if tendering for contracts advertised by the EEC. In general use, the ECU is simply another unit of account along with the various national currencies.

If ECUs are borrowed to finance an investment project in the UK and hence generating income in sterling, then any appreciation of the ECU in terms of sterling may in effect be regarded as an increase in the effective interest cost of the loan. This would be similar to an equal appreciation of say Swiss franc borrowings used to finance sterling earning investments. One way to minimise such risks is to obtain forward cover. Another is to borrow the currency to finance the investment in which the revenue from the investment will be earned. This would be a contra-indication to the use of the ECU.

Status of the ECU in member states

As at July 1983, France, Italy, Ireland and Denmark did not allow residents to hold balances denominated in foreign currencies; this prohibition also applied to the ECU although such deposits were allowed by non-residents. In the Federal Republic of Germany, residents were not allowed to make deposits of ECUs in the country. This reflected German anxieties about the nature of the ECU. No competent monetary authority controls the creation of ECUs and such deposits were held to be a form of indexation of debts that should be denominated in marks. The European Commission believed that the number of individuals holding ECU deposits to be 'quite high' in Belgium and Luxembourg where residents have complete freedom to use foreign deposits.[14]

There were other early indications that suggest an expanding role for the ECU. The Italian government in 1981 decided to give the ECU the status of a fully convertible currency, enabling banks to hold ECU accounts overseas.[15]

By early 1987, progress had been made in a number of areas. British residents had been free to hold ECU deposits since the abolition of exchange control in 1979 and the years since have seen a steady increase in the number of banks offering such facilities. Such deposits are allowed in the Republic of Ireland but the growth of the use of this facility is restricted by the prior need to obtain exchange control permission to buy ECU funds. Such deposits are now allowed in the Federal Republic of Germany. The facility is not widespread. In Lower Saxony, for example, such deposits are only possible with the main branch of one bank, the Norddeutsche Landesbank Centrale. But even this small provision represents considerable progress in the modification of attitudes that date back to the experiences during the hyperinflation of 1923.

The freedom to hold bank balances denominated in the ECU varies in the different countries of the EEC. For example, as at January 1987, citizens of the Irish Republic are not legally prevented from holding ECU denominated accounts but need exchange control permission to exchange the punt for the ECU. In a situation such as this, it is the imposition of exchange control that will restrict the growth of ECU accounts. This is despite the Republic of Ireland being a full member of the European Monetary System. Although the United Kingdom is not a full member, the abolition of exchange control in 1979 has meant that residents may make their own decisions about the extent to which they wish to hold ECU denominated deposits, subject only to any restrictions the commercial banks may impose as to amounts and charges.

The central rate

The determination of the quantities of the national currencies in the ECU basket has been discussed above. Fluctuations in exchange rates between any one currency and the rest of the basket currencies change the value of the ECU in terms of that currency. Defining a central or pivotal value of the ECU in terms of each of the basket currencies that the monetary authorities attempt to maintain over time establishes, for that currency, a central rate of exchange with the ECU.

Changes in the value of the ECU away from the central rates agreed as the pivotal rates of the system reflect fluctuations in the supply of and demand for the individual currencies of the system. These market-determined rates rise and fall over time. Sometimes, during a currency crisis, they may rise and fall rapidly but normally they will fluctuate by a small amount even minute by minute.

Differences in inflation rates, costs and prices, international perceptions of domestic industrial disputes, political strife, interest-rate differentials and speculative movements between currencies all play a part in determining the particular immediate value of one currency in terms of another.

The European Monetary System, with the European Currency Unit (ECU) as its unit of account, has at its heart a set of fixed exchange rates, the central rates, around which the market-determined rates discussed above are supposed to fluctuate within the agreed limits for most of the currencies of $\pm 2.25\%$ either side of the agreed central rate.

Fixing the participating national currencies in terms of the ECU fixes them also in terms of each other, that is, it establishes the set of rates of exchange between all of the individual currencies that the members are then expected to work together to maintain and defend over time. Fixed exchange rates are seen as an expression of the principles of European integration and close cooperation embodied in the Treaty of Rome. Advocates of a fixed rate system see it as an essential prerequisite for the promotion of trade within the Community.

Table 4.2 Central rates revision, January 1987

Currency	Central rate value of the ECU
Belgian franc	42.4582
Danish krone	7.8521
German mark	2.0585
French franc	6.9040
Dutch guilder	2.3194
Irish punt	0.7684
Italian lira	1483.5800

Source: European Commission, Brussels

Table 4.2 shows the central rates prevailing from January 1987. These are not and cannot be fixed for all time. The pressures referred to above build up over time. Failure to totally harmonise domestic economic policies in the member states means balance of payments difficulties due largely to divergent inflation rates and, to a lesser extent, other factors. Although, under this system, high priority is given to maintaining external equilibrium in terms of exchange rate stability, the divergent requirements of internal policies may mean that policies are pursued that create the external problems that lead to pressure for a revision of central rates. Central rates were altered some fourteen times between the introduction of the ECU in 1979 and January 1987.

One must distinguish between a central rate change and a change in the quantities of the national currencies in the ECU itself. There has only been one of these basket revisions, in September 1984. There must be another one in the not too distant future to accommodate the Spanish peseta and Portuguese escudo following the entry of these two countries into the EEC.

As soon as a rate of exchange has been determined between each of the national currencies and the ECU, a central rate between each pair of national currencies is also fixed. As Table 4.2 shows, one ECU is worth both 2.0585 German marks and 6.9040 French francs. This must mean that 2.0585 marks are worth 6.9040 French francs. Thus, one franc must be worth 0.2982 marks and one mark must be worth 3.3539 francs.

Thus, the underlying principle of the European Monetary System is one of fixed exchange rates. With the exception of the lira, the member states agree to maintain the exchange values of their national currencies to within ± 2.25% of the rates implied by the particular set of central rates applying at the time.

Many factors were responsible for the January 1987 changes but the most important was the relationship between the German mark and the French franc. This is summarised in Figure 4.1. The previous set of central rates applying from April 1986 until January 1987 had implied a value of 0.3071 German marks equal to one French franc. By January 1987, the market value of the French franc at 0.3002 marks was the full 2.25% below the parity value set by the central rates. What was to be done?

Action could have been taken in Germany to make the mark less attractive, or in France counterpart action to make the franc more attractive to buyers. This might have involved decreasing German interest rates and increasing French rates and so to harmonise such decisions as to move the exchange rates between the two currencies back towards the parity values set by the April 1986 revision of the central rates.

Both monetary authorities may have been unwilling to have fully adopted these measures; the Germans may have feared an excessive credit expansion if their interest rates were to have been allowed to fall and the French may have feared the deflationary consequences on their domestic economy if the cost of borrowing in France had been allowed to rise.

The alternative in these circumstances is of course to allow the central rates to adjust. This means adjusting the mark upwards against the ECU and the franc downwards, that is, appreciating the mark and depreciating the franc. This will then imply new values of the national currencies in terms of each other with the mark appreciating against the franc. This course of action involves recognising the market rates as a '*fait accompli*' and adjusting new central rates to them.

Such central rate changes are not achieved without negotiation as

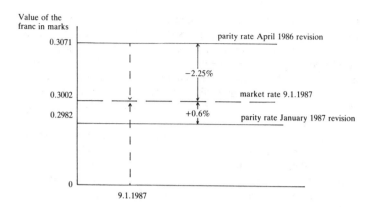

Figure 4.1 Revision of central rates

both countries have an interest in the value of each other's currency in terms of its own. A depreciating French franc will increase French competitiveness in German markets and make it more difficult for the Germans to sell in France.

It was this latter alternative that was reflected in the central rate changes of January 1987. What actually happened between the franc and the mark is summarised in Figure 4.1. The 'weak' French franc has been made 'strong' by altering the parity rate between the two currencies. The judgement of the market has been accepted! Whereas the franc was 2.25% below its previous parity value of 0.3071 marks, it is now 0.06% above the new parity rate of 0.2982 marks.

In effect, when divergences in rates of exchange from the central rates become so large that it is impossible to contemplate the introduction of the necessary domestic policies to bring the rates back towards the central rates, discussions take place to establish a new set of central rates that in effect move towards the values currently being established in the foreign exchange markets.

Such changes are discussed at the highest levels within the Community. This would normally involve meetings of finance ministers. It is easy to see why such decisions are extremely political in nature. The commitment to a particular set of exchange rates had important consequences for the participants. To allow one currency to depreciate against the ECU and hence against other national currencies means that the country with the depreciating currency is allowed to gain an export advantage over other member states. To push a country towards accepting an appreciation of its currency means that it is being asked to lose a financially competitive edge in its export trade. It is thus likely to find pressure against such changes from domestic interests that stand to lose out from particular changes.

A sign that the European economies were integrating more closely in monetary matters would be if central rate changes were becoming smaller and less frequent. This is not happening. More closely integrated decision making is taking place but this has not yet been reflected in a need for smaller, less frequent rate changes.

The parity grid

As discussed above, fixing the values of the currencies of the member states in relation to the ECU also fixes them in relation to each other. If the implied rates of exchange are set out as in Table 4.3, we derive the parity grid of exchange rates. These are all derived by simple arithmetic from the central rates applying from January 1987.

Table 4.3 Parity grid

	Belgian franc	Danish krone	German mark
Belgian franc	1.0000	0.1849	0.0485
Danish krone	5.44072	1.0000	0.2622
German mark	20.6255	3.8144	1.0000

This grid is not complete and is shown by way of illustration of the principles involved in its construction. To complete the grid would involve extending it to include the currencies of the other member states participating fully in the European Monetary System (EMS).

In January 1987, this would mean extending it to include the national currencies of France, Holland, Ireland and Italy. The currencies of the United Kingdom, Greece, Spain and Portugal would be excluded as these countries do not as yet commit themselves fully to the EMS by agreeing to fix the exchange rates between their currencies and those of the other member states within agreed limits.

Exchange rate movements

Full membership of the EMS requires that members work together to maintain the parity grid rates and also the value of the ECU in terms of each of the national currencies.

Consider as an example of what is involved in this double commitment the German mark. From January 1987, inspection of the parity grid rates in the table indicates that the central target rate to be maintained against the Danish krone is one mark equal to 3.8144 krone with the rules of the EMS allowing for a range around this value of $\pm$ 2.25%. This means a lower permissible limit of 3.8144–0.0858 = 3.7286 krone and an upper limit of 3.8144 + 0.0858 = 3.9002 krone.

What about the German mark in relation to the ECU? Its central rate from January 1987 was 2.05853 marks equal to one ECU. The limits to the fluctuations in value around this central rate cannot be calculated as simply the central rate value $\pm$ 2.25%.

This is because the mark itself is part of the ECU. The 1984 revision of the basket had included 0.719 of a mark. With the January 1987 revision of the central rates establishing an ECU as worth 2.05853 marks, this means that the mark is now 0.719/2.05853 = 34.928% of the unit.

The mark can only vary against the non-mark constituents of the ECU. This means that it can vary not by the full $\pm$ 2.25% but by (1–0.34928)x2.25%, that is, by $\pm$ 1.46412%. This may be easier to appreciate if one considers extreme values. If the mark were to be identical with the ECU, then no variation would be possible, the value of the expression in the brackets above would then be zero. If the mark did not form part of the ECU, then the full 2.25% variation would be possible, the value of the expression in brackets would then be equal to one. This is important later in the chapter in the discussion of the meaning of printed information commonly published on the ECU.

Table 4.4 Calculation of divergence values for EMS currencies

Currency	ECU basket from 17.9.1984	% of ECU	% other currencies	Maximum divergence against ECU %	Divergence limit or threshold
(1)	(2)	(3)	(4)	(5)	(6)
German mark	0.719 DM	34.928	65.072	±1.4641	±1.0981
Dutch guilder	0.256 DG	11.037	88.963	±2.0017	±1.5012
Belgian franc	3.85 BF	9.068	90.932	±2.0460	±1.5344
Danish krone	0.219 DK	2.789	97.211	±2.1872	±1.6404
French franc	1.31 FF	18.975	81.025	±1.8231	±1.3674
Irish punt	0.0087 IP	1.134	98.866	±2.2245	±1.6684
Italian lira	140.00 L	9.437	90.563	±5.4338	±4.0752

Information required to follow developments in the European Monetary System

The statistics required to follow developments within the exchange rate structure of the European Monetary System are implied by the previous discussion. A statement of the current central rates, the actual rates in terms of the ECU day by day, and various measurements of the divergences between these rates for each of the participating currencies are suggested.

Central rates and daily values of the ECU, in terms of not only the national currencies of those member states of the Community fully participating in the EMS but also of several other currencies, are published by the European Commission. Table 4.4 is restricted to the currencies of those countries fully participating in the EMS.

The table may be readily understood from the fully worked example for the German mark considered above. The reasoning is repeated for the French franc. The present ECU basket contains 1.31 FF with a central rate value of 6.9040 FF equal to one ECU. Thus, the French franc equals $(1.31/6.9040)100\% = 18.975\%$ of one ECU. All other currencies thus constitute 81.025% of one ECU.

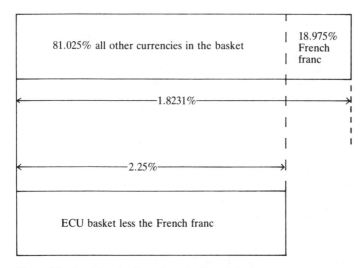

Figure 4.2 Applying the formula to the French franc

The French franc may vary by ± 2.25% against all the other currencies of the ECU. It may vary thus by 81.025% of 2.25% against the ECU of which it is itself part. Thus, it may vary as a maximum against the ECU by ± 1.8231%.

Column (5) values are thus obtained by multiplying column (4) values by 2.25% with the exception of the data relating to the Italian lira. As the lira is allowed a wider range of fluctuation of ±6.000%, the column (5) value for this currency is obtained by multiplying the column (4) value by the wider value allowed.

Figure 4.2 may help to make this particular point clearer. No currency in the ECU basket can vary against itself, it can only vary in its exchange value against the other currencies of the basket. Thus, variation against the ECU is restricted by this particular rigidity.

The position of the French franc in this respect is discussed above. It is summarised in the diagram. A maximum allowed variation against the ECU minus the French franc of ±2.25% is reduced to a maximum of ±1.8231 against the entire ECU unit including the franc.

A general formula may be deduced from this argument. It is

$$
\begin{pmatrix}
\text{Permissible vari-} \\
\text{ations against the} \\
\text{ECU for any cur-} \\
\text{rency in the 'basket'} \\
\text{and fully par-} \\
\text{ticipating in the} \\
\text{EMS}
\end{pmatrix}
=
\begin{pmatrix}
\text{Per-} \\
\text{centage of} \\
1 - \text{the basket} \\
\text{comprising} \\
\text{any cur-} \\
\text{rency}
\end{pmatrix}
\times
\begin{pmatrix}
(2.25\% \text{ for all} \\
\text{fully par-} \\
\text{ticipating cur-} \\
\text{renies except} \\
\text{the lira. } 6\% \\
\text{for the lira})
\end{pmatrix}
$$

The values in column (5) of Table 4.4 are all maximum variation limits under the rules of the EMS. As part of the way the system works, lower values set at 75% of the maximum variations allowed are indicated as points at which policies should be introduced to prevent wider variations developing. It is these values that are listed in column (6). Column (6) values are all 75% of the corresponding column (5) values. Thus, for the German mark, ± 1.0981% is 75% of ± 1.4641%.

Following published financial information on the ECU is now relatively straightforward. We may now detect strain in the EMS by

Table 4.5 Deviation of market values of ECU from central rates

Currency (1)	ECU central rates (2)	Market value of the ECU 13.1.1987 (3)	% change from central rate (4)	Divergence limit (5)
Belgian franc	42.4582	42.7596	+0.71%	±1.5344
French franc	6.9040	6.8985	−0.08%	±1.3674
German mark	2.0585	2.0622	+0.18%	±1.0891

Source: *Financial Times*, 14 January 1987

comparing, for each country, the deviation of the market value of the ECU in terms of its currency from its central rate, to either the maximum permissible deviation or to the divergence limit.

An example of this is shown in Table 4.5. It is limited to three of the currencies fully participating in the EMS for illustration only. Inspection of the table shows that the Belgian franc has depreciated against the ECU, that is, the price of an ECU in terms of the Belgian franc has risen. There are two ways of measuring the differences between central rates and market rates. We may either, as in the table, show the changes for the ECU against the particular currency, or for the currency against the ECU. The choice will determine the sign. In this example, the Belgian franc is relatively weak compared to its central rate. The ECU has appreciated (+) by 0.71%. The Belgian franc has depreciated (-) by 0.71%. It is simply a question of choice which method we choose to measure the divergence.

The next step is to compare columns (4) and (5). Column (5) shows the divergence values at which intervention under the rules is supposed to be triggered. Thus, a comparison of (4) and (5) indicates how likely it is that we are at or are nearing a 'crisis' in the EMS.

It is not enough simply to compare the numerical values in these two columns. What is also important is the speed with which column (4) values approach the limits of column (5). The judgement may well be that the EMS is performing much better according to its own criteria if the divergence limits were approached say 2 years after the last central rate revisions rather than after only say 1 month.

The ECU market is different in many respects from the markets for foreign currencies generally. For example, the market rates displayed in the tables in this chapter are set by the European Commission in Brussels on a daily basis. The central bank of each member state sends a 'representative' rate of its currency in terms of the United States dollar to the National Bank of Belgium, thence to the Commission which 'uses them to calculate an ECU equivalent first in dollars and then in the currencies of the member states'.[16]

Following divergences over time

We may track divergences for one currency over time or arrange the diagram in such a way as to enable the behaviour of divergences for several currencies to be compared. Figure 4.3 considers the Belgian franc alone and Figure 4.4 arranges the information in such a way as to enable it to be compared to the German mark and the Danish krone.

As market rates are published daily in Brussels, so Figure 4.3 may be plotted on a daily basis. If the current arrangement of rates is 'working well' then market rates will fluctuate around the central

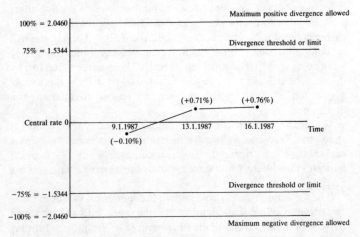

Figure 4.3 Deviation of the Belgian franc from ECU central rate compared to its maximum divergence spread

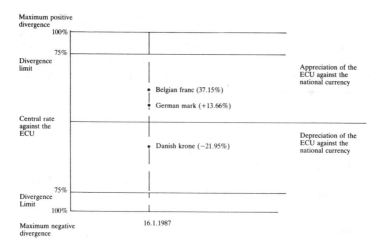

Figure 4.4 Divergence over time

rate value or around the horizontal axis in the Figure. It is the persistent tendencies for divergences to head towards the limits that reflects the inability of the EMS to hold to a particular set of central rates indefinitely.

Following divergences over time – several currencies simultaneously
Consider the values in Table 4.6 for three of the currencies fully participating in the EMS. The figures in column (4) measure the deviations of market rates from central rates as percentages of the maximum deviations allowed under the rules of the EMS and reflect the weights of the individual currencies in the ECU basket.

Table 4.6 Simultaneous divergencies of currencies

Currency	Divergence from central rates 16.1.1987	Maximum divergence allowed	(3) as % of (2) (4)
Danish krone	−0.48	±2.1872	− 21.95
German mark	+0.20	±1.4641	+ 13.66
Belgian franc	+0.76	±2.0460	+ 37.15

Column (4) values will vary from day to day and by plotting successive daily values for the currencies fully participating in the EMS, the eye can follow the performance of the system.

Figure 4.4 is maintained over time as part of the statistical services provided by the European Community's Statistical Service in Luxembourg. Plotting these values on a daily basis enables the eye to easily follow the path of divergence of any currency relative to any other over time.[17]

It may be misleading to interpret successful operation of the EMS in terms of how closely around zero the series fluctuate. As departures from zero become larger, a realignment of central rates will reduce the disparities and show up in a return towards zero divergence. This might be missed on the diagram unless marked.

Notes

1 'On the international monetary convention and the introduction of an international currency into this kingdom', W. S. Jevons. Read before the Manchester Statistical Society, 13 May 1868. Published in *Transactions of the Manchester Statistical Society*, 1867–8, pp. 79–92.

2 Written Question 1810/82, *Official Journal of the European Communities*, C111/10 25 April 1983.

3 Written Question 1811/82, *Official Journal of the European Communities*, C125/26 9 May 1983.

4 Bremen meeting in 1978 that established the European Monetary System.

5 D. Stresser, *The Finances of Europe*, Commission of the European Communities, Luxembourg, 1980, inside cover.

6 *23rd Report on the Activities of the Monetary Committee*, European Commission, 1982, p. 7.

7 *Fifth Report. House of Lords European Communities Committee. Session 1983–1984*, EMS (HL 39), HMSO.

8 For example, if an exporter sells to the United States, he may expect to be paid in US dollars in, say, 6 months' time. It is uncertain what the exchange rate with sterling will be at that time. Thus, the sterling equivalent of the expected future delivery of dollars is uncertain. A bank will, however, commit itself to buying these dollars when received at an exchange rate agreed now. This is an example of forward cover provided, for a fee, by a bank. It is at its most expensive, like all insurance, when most needed, which is when rates are fluctuating and it is most difficult to forecast future currency values.

9   'Implications of European Monetary Union', *Economist*, 5 August 1972, pp. 56–7.

10   For example, Article 3(g) provides for the activities of the European Commission 'to include the application of procedures by which the economic policies of Member States can be coordinated and disequilibria in their balances of payments remedied'.

11   *The Private Uses of the ECU*, Kredietbank, Brussels, 1980.

12   *ECU (European Currency Unit)*, Lloyds Bank PLC, Overseas Division, May 1982, p. 5.

13   *Lloyds Bank International Financial Outlook*, No. 10, January 1983, pp. 2–3.

14   See answer given on behalf of the European Commission to Written Question 2128/83. Official Journal C177/10, 5 July 1983.

15   *Lloyds Bank International Financial Outlook*, No. 10, January 1983, p. 2.

16   See *Eurostat Money and Finance*, 4th Qtr., 1984, p. 9, published by the Statistical Service of the European Community, Luxembourg.

17   *Eurostat Money and Finance*. Published quarterly and containing a table covering movements in the divergence indicators as discussed above, published by European Community's Statistical Service, Luxembourg.

Chapter Five

The evaluation of a company

Companies constitute a major part of and play an important role in the financial system of the UK. Much of the information derived from such sources as company reports and the media summarising their activities relates to financial performance. Data relating to profitability and dividend policy is considered in this chapter.

Other financial information assesses the sensitivity of companies to outside factors such as changes in Stock Market conditions generally. Something of the randomness of index levels is considered, suggesting that the level of a particular share price is not solely determined by factors intrinsic to the company.

Earnings per share

The earnings of a company are simply the net profit after tax attributable to the ordinary shareholders of the company. The concept is easy to define but not necessarily so easy to calculate. The concept of earnings occurs on a number of occasions in this chapter.

The total earnings of a company appear in the annual published accounts of the company. In the summary information published after each year's trading, this figure is more often reported as earnings per share (EPS). Thus, in this chapter, we note total earnings of £114m for the Midland Bank or 60.6p per ordinary share. Dividing the former by the latter shows there to be some 188,118,810 ordinary shares making up the issued share capital of the Midland Bank. For Cadbury Schweppes PLC, we note an earnings per share figure of 13.60p.

The earnings of a company are clearly of interest to shareholders and to investors considering the merits of investment in one company rather than another. Apart from an interest *per se* in the profitability of the company, the earnings figure is of importance in the calculation of certain statistics used in the analysis of the performance of the company. The figure for earnings is important in the calculation of the price earnings ratio and the dividend cover ratio. These are both key statistics reported daily in the financial press and considered in detail later in the chapter. Some of the problems that arise in the definition and calculation of earnings per share are now discussed.

Earnings are important as the source of finance for dividends, for the internal financing of future investment and growth, and its changing value over time is a measure of the progress and efficiency of the company and the effectiveness of its management.

Earnings per share have already been defined as the profits after tax attributable to the ordinary shareholders of the company divided by the total number of ordinary shares.

Table 5.1 Example of earnings per share

		Year One	Year Two
(1)	Profit after tax attributable to the ordinary shareholders	£400,000	£625,000
(2)	Number of ordinary shares	4,000,000	5,000,000
(3)	Earnings per share = (1)/(2)	10p	12.5p

We notice in our example (Table 5.1) an increase of 25% in the earnings per share from the one set of annual accounts to the next. The relevant growth figure is not only reported in the annual accounts but may well be press advertised by the company itself as part of its image-building campaign with the public. Unfortunately, reality is seldom so simple. Actual real-world calculations of earnings per share are more complex for a number of reasons.

The relationship between earnings net of tax and the dividend policy pursued by the company is probably the most important problem to grasp in order to understand published financial data.

Certain taxation liabilities are not affected by dividend policy.

Corporation tax, taxation on dividends received and overseas tax unrelieved because the rate of overseas tax exceeds the rate of UK Corporation Tax, are fixed in the sense that they are independent of the actual dividend policy pursued. They are also constant company by company.

Other taxation is dependent upon dividend policy. Examples are irrecoverable Advanced Corporation Tax (ACT) and overseas tax unrelieved because dividend payments restrict the available double tax credit. These are variable company to company.

It would be misleading if earnings per share varied from one year to the next, not because the profitability of the company was changing, but because the company had altered its dividend policy.

If the company were to distribute nothing in the way of dividends, then the variable dividend-related deductions would be zero. It is thus possible to calculate earnings per share, not by actually distributing nothing as dividends, but by assuming that nothing had been distributed.

The earnings per share so calculated yields the so-called *nil* basis of estimation of earnings per share. It does not mean that the variable tax items (dividend policy dependent) are not incurred. It means that they are ignored in the computation of EPS. As the company may have paid the variable items, the EPS as calculated may not be the actual earnings of the company, that is, the net profit remaining after all tax has been paid. Where the EPS is calculated on the nil basis and variable tax items are paid, such an EPS will be larger by the amount of these items than the actual EPS controlled by the company.

Some authors see this nil basis as the preferred method of calculating EPS. It has the advantage of treating companies as if they were in the same tax environment, although they may pursue quite different dividend policies. One criterion of an 'ideal' EPS is that it should permit inter-company comparisons and should not be affected by dividend payment policies.

Such an after-tax net profit per share value is reached only by ignoring those tax differences that reflect the differing extent to which companies are engaged in overseas trade and ignoring likewise tax differences that relate to differing dividend policies.

It is clear that this basis of calculating EPS may be objected to. It overstates EPS for those companies paying irrecoverable ACT and unrelieved overseas tax. Overstating the EPS may make a company look more attractive to an investor than otherwise would be the case.

An estimate of EPS may thus be preferable that shows a figure net of all tax liabilities actually incurred, whether it be dividend policy, unrelieved overseas tax or irrecoverable ACT.

Such a figure is called the EPS on the *net* basis, that is, net of all taxes incurred for whatever reasons. This basis of calculation results in a figure of net profit that is actually available for the individual company to allocate to dividends, reserves, capital formation, or whatever. The net basis is the basis of calculation required for Stock Exchange listed companies in the UK. It is a listing requirement. It is also the considered requirement of the accountancy profession.[1]

The disadvantages of this method of calculation are clear. Differences in EPS between companies may form the basis of differential judgements about the managerial efficiencies in the companies being compared. Yet, as the discussion above makes clear, net basis figures for EPS reflect the different taxation environments in which the companies operate by virtue of a different degree of involvement in foreign trade and as a result of pursuing different dividend policies.

Thus, the EPS figures generally reported in the financial press are, unless otherwise stated, calculated on the net basis. They are sometimes shown bracketed to indicate that a nil basis estimate would yield an EPS figure 10% or more greater than the printed net basis estimates.

It is also possible to calculate earnings per share in a third way as if all the earnings had been distributed as dividends and Advanced Corporation Tax paid. This notional tax may not be totally recoverable when Corporation Tax is paid, that is, it may exceed the actual taxation due. Thus, earnings per share may be lower on this *maximum distribution basis* (MDB) assumption than on either the nil or net assumptions discussed above.

Printed cover ratio figures are estimated on the basis of the maximum distribution assumption and will thus be lower than such ratios calculated directly from the company's annual accounts that are drawn up on the net basis. This point is taken up below in the discussion of the nature and interpretation of the various commonly reported ratios.

Table 5.2 Earnings per share summary

Basis of calculation	Assumption	Advantages	Disadvantages
Net basis	Dividend policy assumed is the policy actually adopted by the company	The EPS figure is the amount actually earned by the company and is available for disposal	Direct meaningful comparison with the EPS of another company in a different tax environment is made difficult and is not directly and readily possible.
Nil basis	Dividend policy assumed is that nothing has been distributed as dividends	The figure is directly comparable to the figures calculated for other companies on the same basis. A more meaningful comparison is thus possible between companies pursuing different dividend policies	The EPS figure is not the figure corresponding to the net profit per share actually available to the company.
Maximum distribution basis	It is assumed that all the earnings have been distributed as dividends and taxation paid accordingly.	A conservative estimate of earnings is produced. Used in printed cover ratio data in the financial press	The figure produced is different from the EPS actually available to the company.

The problem of dilution

Table 5.2 summarises the three ways discussed of calculating earnings per share. It must be remembered that the value of the EPS figure is calculated by *dividing total earnings* by the total number of ordinary shares. The NET, NIL and MAXIMUM DISTRIBUTION bases of estimation all refer to different assumptions underlying the calculations of the numerator of the relevant fraction, that is, the relevant total figure attributable to the ordinary shareholders. Earnings per share can of course vary depending upon what assumptions we care to make about the denominator of the fraction, that is, the relevant figure for the total number of ordinary shares.

A company may be aware of an intention to increase the equity of the company, that is, increase the number of ordinary shares that rank for dividend. This will have the effect of reducing or diluting the earnings per share below what they otherwise would be by increasing the denominator of the equation.

A figure for *fully diluted earnings* may thus be calculated. The numerator remains normally the total earnings attributable to the ordinary shareholders calculated on the net basis. The denominator is then not the actual number of shares currently issued but the anticipated future total in the next accounting period given the additional shares it is expected to issue.

Good practice requires the publication of such *fully diluted earnings* if the effect of future intended expansions of the equity would decrease the EPS by 5% or more. There may well be a protest from existing equity holders if a proposal to increase the number of ordinary shares would be likely to 'excessively' dilute the EPS.

Such protests have been voiced at the time of writing about the dilution of the equity of the Dunlop Group. This group is in severe financial difficulties, having sold off its tyre production facilities at its Birmingham plant to the Japanese company Sumitomo but is still left with large debts owing to banks and other financial institutions. A recent proposal is to financially reconstruct the company by converting the financial sums owing to creditors into ordinary shares of the company. This proposal would have the effect of significantly diluting the earnings per share and thus the interests of the existing holders of Dunlop equity. In this particular case, however, there is the counterweight of the argument that, if the company is not reconstructed and goes bankrupt without hope of rescue, then the existing shareholders will have lost everything, not just a dilution of the EPS.

Some other problems with the denominator

The appropriate figure for the number of ordinary shares that should be used in an EPS calculation is not simply the number of shares outstanding at the beginning or the end of the accounting period. The number of shares may well change during the year because of capitalisation issues, share exchanges and rights issues.[2]

Consider the following problem:

Profits for the year after tax	£ 535,000
Number of ordinary shares ranking for dividend 1 Jan.	1,000,000
Number of ordinary shares ranking for dividend 1 Apr.	1,200,000

What is the EPS in this company?

A weighted average calculation is clearly required. One million shares constituted the ordinary shares of the company for 90 days and 1,200,000 for 275 days. The calculation set out below should be clear from the discussion above on the properties of weighted indices.

$$
\text{Earnings per share (in pence per share)} = \frac{535,000 \times 100}{[90/365(1,000,000) + 275/365(1,200,000)]}
$$

$$
= \frac{535,000 \times 100}{1,150,684.8}
$$

$$
= 46.49
$$

Notice that 1,150,684.8 is the weighted average number of ordinary shares outstanding. The 'easy' average of 1,100,000 would only be accurate if the 20% increase in the equity had taken place exactly halfway through the year. For a more detailed consideration of other problems of defining an appropriate denominator, the reader is referred to the reference in Note 1.

The first part of this chapter has considered the nature and calculation of the earnings per share of a company. This was partly by way of a lead in to a consideration of the published data commonly reported in the financial press relating to a company's financial position. The second part of this chapter now considers the published information in some detail.

Types of commonly published information

Public limited companies (PLCs) publish annual accounts and reports to the shareholders, the form and detail of which are determined by the provisions of the Companies Acts and the listing requirements of the Stock Exchange. The latter requires certain presentational criteria to be met in return for a listing, that is, in return for trading in the shares of the company to take place on the Stock Exchange.

Thus, the form of the annual accounts that appears in summary form in the financial press is also determined by the need to meet these requirements. The group accounts for the financial year ended 31 December 1983 for the Midland Bank and Cadbury Schweppes shown below take the form indicated as a result of the operation of these criteria.

We begin by showing the form of the commonly published information for these two groups and then proceed to consider the interpretation of the data.

Example One

Midland Bank Group results for the year ended 31 December 1983

Trading profit before bad debts	£612m
Profit before taxation	£225m
Attributable profit	£114m
Earnings per share (Net)	60.6p
Dividend per share	25.5p

Source: Annual Accounts and Report to Shareholders

On 21 March 1984, the data relating to the Midland Bank Group printed in the financial press was as follows:

	Price	Net dividend	Cover	Gross yield	P/E
Midland Bank	387p x.d.	25.5p	2.1	9.4	6.4

Source: *Financial Times*, 21.3.1984

Example Two

Cadbury Schweppes results for the year ended 31 December 1983

Trading profits	125.6m
Profit before tax	106.9m
Earnings per share (Net)	13.60p
Dividends per share	5.4p

Again on the 21st March 1984, the data relating to Cadbury Schweppes printed in the financial press was as follows

	Price	Net dividend	Cover	Gross yield	P/E
Cadbury Schweppes	128p	5.4p	1.9	6.02%	9.4

Source: *Financial Times*, 21.3.1984

Earnings per share calculated on the net basis does not strictly permit inter-company comparisons but it does have the advantage that the figure is meaningful in the sense that it equals money available to the company apart from that distributed as dividends.

Earnings per share calculated on the nil or maximum distribution basis are constructs that assume dividend policies different from the dividend policies actually pursued. The imposition of one of these 'extreme' assumptions about dividend policy enables inter-company comparisons to be made as it then eliminates taxation differences that reflect different dividend policies. Thus, EPS figures then are more comparable between companies. Actual dividend policy will normally of course lie between these extremes, that is, between the zero dividend assumption of the nil basis and the 100% dividend of the MDB. If either of these extreme assumptions is made, the EPS figure calculated is only a statistic permitting inter-company comparisons on the basis of a common assumption it is not a figure that represents money actually available to the company.

In practice, the numerical difference between EPS on the net and nil bases is generally less than 10% for most listed companies. Standard practice in most financial newspapers such as the *Financial Times* is to bracket P/E ratios if the nil and net bases of calculation would yield a difference of 10% or more in the numerical values of the ratio. This would be of course a difference of 10% or more in the value of the denominator of the ratio, the figure for the EPS of the company. A glance at the Stock Exchange columns of the *Financial Times* on 8 November 1984 showed some 187 bracketed. Thus, some 187 EPS figures would have been 10% or more apart on a comparison using the nil and net bases. It is thus a relatively small number that diverge by 10% or more depending on the basis of calculation. Thus, subject to realising that unbracketed figures may conceal variations up to 10% and that the published net basis figures may make one company look relatively less efficient than another simply due to taxation differences that affect EPS due to different dividend policies, the net basis figures may in practice be used with caution to assess companies against one another.

The maximum distribution basis figure for EPS is of major practical significance in that it is the numerator of the cover ratio published in the *Financial Times*. The advantages and disadvantages of its use for this purpose are discussed later when the cover ratio is considered.

The principal taxation of company profits in the United Kingdom is Corporation Tax. This tax takes two forms, Advanced Corporation Tax and Mainstream Corporation Tax.

Advanced Corporation tax is paid whenever a dividend payment is made at a rate equal to the standard rate of income tax currently prevailing, 30% for the period to which these accounts relate.[3] Thus, with a net dividend of 25.5p per ordinary share, the Midland Bank would have paid to the Inland Revenue ACT of 10.9p per share and Cadbury Schweppes on a net dividend of 5.4p would have paid ACT of 2.3p per share. These amounts are the sums shown as tax credits on the dividend form received by the shareholder. The amount of ACT paid is thus determined by the company's dividend policy, the larger the net dividend, the greater the amount paid by the company to the Inland Revenue. It will be observed that the gross dividend payment is divided 70/30[4] between the net dividend payment and the ACT payment. The reader is invited to check that the figures given above for the Midland Bank and Cadbury Schweppes satisfy this ratio.[5]

Mainstream Corporation Tax (MCT) is paid later in time than Advanced Corporation Tax at the rate, for the period to which these accounts relate, of 52%. Compared to the ACT rate of 30%, this might lead the unsuspecting to assume that offset ACT against MCT would leave a balance owing to the Inland Revenue. If this were so, ACT would be less than MCT and dividend policy would not determine the total taxation payable, only the timing of the various components of the total tax bill. Furthermore, in this situation, EPS would be independent of dividend policy and ACT would make only a partial prepayment of the final tax bill. ACT is of course only recoverable if it is smaller than the final tax bill.[6]

However, many companies pay little or no Mainstream Corporation Tax and thus have no tax liability against which Advanced Corporation Tax may be offset. It has been estimated, for example, that such household names as Allied Lyons, Courtaulds, the Ford Motor Co. and ICI paid no MCT in the tax year 1981/2.[7] This arises because companies are permitted to deduct interest on loans and the use of profit for investment finance before arriving at the tax base figure.

They must however pay ACT which is not then recoverable if there is no MCT charge. Thus, in these cases, dividend policy determines taxation and hence EPS.

EPS calculated on the MDB will thus yield the smallest figure in these cases and EPS on the NIL basis the highest figure with an intermediate value for NET basis calculations.

Net dividend and gross yield

The net dividend is reported in the company's annual accounts and in the financial press daily. It is a constant figure until the next dividend payment is declared. Yields depend upon the share price as well as upon the dividend payment. As the price of a share may well vary day by day, the related yield figure is also varying daily and can only thus be found in the financial press and not in the annual accounts of the company.

A net yield is very simply calculated. Divide the net dividend by the current share price and multiply the quotient by 100 to yield the net figure as a percentage.

Using the Cadbury Schweppes data, the net yield is thus

$$\frac{(5.4 \times 100)}{128} = 4.22\%$$

Using the Midland Bank data, the net dividend yield calculation is thus:

$$\frac{(25.5 \times 100)}{387} = 6.59\%$$

There are a number of points to note about these calculations. First, the yield calculated is only net of standard rate tax of 30%.[8] It would be reduced further for taxpayers holding these shares paying rates of tax higher than the standard rate. Thus, it is not a particularly useful yield to publish. It is of much more general value to publish a yield gross, that is, before any tax has been deducted. The individual taxpayer can then calculate his own net return by deducting his own top marginal rate of tax.

The denominator needs careful interpretation. The closing price printed in the financial press is normally the average of the closing selling and buying prices. As may be seen by consulting the *Stock Exchange Daily List*, the closing selling price may well be some 10p above the printed price in the daily newspaper and the closing buying price some 10p below. Thus, printed yield figures are themselves simple arithmetic averages of the two yield figures that would be produced by using both the closing prices from the *Daily List*. The printed figure is thus higher than a buyer of the shares would get if he were to acquire them at the closing buying price of the previous day and is lower than that given up by the seller who sells at the closing selling price.

Between dividend payments, yields fluctuate as prices change whereas the numerator remains constant. The calculation is based on the last dividend paid. This is not available to the present purchaser. What interests him is the yield represented by the next dividend payment, a matter normally of some conjecture. Such prospective yields may well bear a very uncertain relationship to the yield calculated using the last dividend payment and the current share price.

This section explores the links between the net dividend and gross yield figures published in the financial press. A net dividend figure in pence per share and a gross yield as a percentage are normally published.

The first step is to add back the Advanced Corporation Tax that was deducted from the gross dividend payment. This 'adding back' is also known as 'grossing up' at the standard rate of income tax as ACT is levied at this rate.

Let x be the net dividend as an amount in pence per share and y the gross dividend again as an amount in pence per share. Now $0.7y = x$ where tax is deducted at the standard rate of 0.30 or 30%. Thus, $x/0.7 = y$ or $(10/7)x = y$. This becomes:

$$\text{Gross dividend } (y) = \frac{10 \times \text{Net dividend in pence per share } (x)}{7}$$

Given the standard rate of tax of 30%, the required multiplier to be applied to the net dividend to yield the gross dividend is thus $10/7$.

By formula, the gross yield is related to the net dividend as follows:

$$\frac{\text{Gross yield}}{\text{(as published)}} = \frac{\text{Net dividend (p)} \times 100 \times 10}{\text{Share price (p)} \times 7}$$

The net dividend share price gives the net yield as a proportion. Multiplying by 100 converts the net dividend as a proportion into net dividend as a percentage. The $10/7$ is the multiplier that converts the net yield into a gross yield allowing for tax at the standard rate of 30% prevailing at the time these calculations were made.[9]

Example: *Cadbury Schweppes Data*

Substituting the data into the formula;

Gross yield $= \dfrac{\text{Net dividend (p)} \times 100 \times 10}{\text{Share price (p)} \times 7}$

$= \dfrac{5.4 \times 100 \times 10}{128 \times 7}$

$= 6.02\%$

This figure should be compared to the published data on Cadbury Schweppes trading for the year ended 31 December 1983 and the published information on the company in the *Financial Times* for the 21 March 1984 printed above. The calculation above shows how the net dividend of 5.4p per share, the share price of 128p, and the published gross yield of 6.02% are related to each other.

Example: *Midland Bank Group Data*

Substituting the data into the same formula as for Cadbury Schweppes in the previous example produces the following:

Gross yield $= \dfrac{25.5\text{p} \times 100 \times 10}{387 \times 7}$

$= 9.4\%$

Comparing these figures to the published data given earlier in this chapter, it will be seen that the calculation shows how the net dividend of 25.5p is related to the share price of 387p to produce the gross yield of 9.4%.

The formula may be used to check the commonly published data. Modifying it slightly and using the price one has paid oneself for the particular share will enable the gross yield to be calculated as it applies to one's own portfolio holdings of the share. This may well be radically different from published yields that relate to current prices for shares that were acquired at significantly different prices from those prevailing at the present time.

Chapter 1 on gilt-edged securities devoted some time to a discussion about the nature of 'accrued interest' and the reasons for stripping it from the published gilt price to obtain a suitable denominator for yield calculations. This is not done for equity yield arithmetic but the same principle applies. The price of a particular share will tend to rise towards the next dividend payment in anticipation of that dividend. The expected dividend will be discounted into the present price of the share. No precise arithmetical calculation would be possible as, unlike a fixed interest coupon gilt, the next dividend is inevitably partly a matter of opinion and conjecture. The analogous drop in price to represent dividend forgone when the share goes exdividend is also, other things being equal, noticeable. Suffice it to record that the principles involved are identical but no notice of it is taken in yield calculations on equities.

Comparisons of gross yield
Should we go for an investment in the stock offering the highest published gross yield? It has its immediate attractions but the answer must be not necessarily.

A relatively low yield may indicate a number of characteristics pointing in different directions in so far as the attractiveness of the share to the potential investor is concerned.

The yield may be relatively low because the earnings per share from which the dividend is to be paid are relatively low and thus indicate a relatively unattractive stock. It may also be low because the company pursues a conservative dividend policy paying out in this way only a very small percentage of relatively high earnings. A low dividend paying stock may attract a high stock market price because it is regarded as a growth stock. It may be thus bought for its future capital growth potential and current dividends may play only a minor role in determining its current price. Thus, if we are looking for growth in future capital values, we may feel that this is more to be found in stocks with a currently rather low yield.

Relatively high yielding equities may be high yielding because they are established well managed companies but not companies thought to be exploiting new growth promoting technologies.

Rewards are thus to be sought more immediately in the yield rather than in future growth.

Thus, either presently high or low yielding stocks may be sought depending upon the investor's personal preference for income or capital growth allied to what he thinks the present yields indicate about the future of the company's growth and profitability.

With equities, we are in a much more uncertain world than with British government securities. With the latter, all future dividend payments to maturity are known from the coupon rates.[10] The amount of capital growth between purchase and redemption is also known for dated stocks. The purchase price and allied costs of acquisition are known, as is the redemption value and date of the stock. It is thus a matter of arithmetic to annualise the difference into a rate of capital change. For equities, there is no such certainty. The future capital growth is uncertain and may be badly misjudged by the market. A first-class growth stock may become the stock to be avoided at all costs, the stock of a bankrupt company. The recent example of the London and Liverpool Trust PLC[11] is a salutary reminder of the perils in buying equities on the promise of future profits on the expected successful exploitation of a market leading product.

This company failed because of the failure of its scheme to sell video juke boxes to public houses. The Receiver was called in in May 1984 when bank debts incurred had increased to £7m. Yet the price had risen from a 1980 low of 27.5p to a 1982 high of 410p, surely the meteoric price rise of a growth stock if there ever was one. Such rapid price rises pull down yields but are only justified in the long run if the earnings per share 'catch up' with the price and future profitability warrants the present high price.

Another example of a cautionary tale is the price history of the ordinary shares of Polly Peck (Holdings) PLC. From a 'low' of 5.5p per share in 1980, this company's ordinary shares rose to a high of £36 in 1983 to fall back to a low for that year of £9. It looks very much that over-enthusiastic buying waves lead to price levels that are unrealistic in the light of any conceivable potential increase in earnings and associated dividends. Market recognition of this then causes a relatively sudden sharp drop in price as the correction takes place. Beware then of reading too much into a particular price in relationship to its trend for some time past–it may be due for a sudden sharp reversal.

The yield figures published in the financial press focus on the relationship between the price of the share at the moment and the dividend last paid. It is thus a highly dividend-sensitive statistic.

We may be more interested in the relationship between the price of the share at the moment and the earnings per share as revealed in the last accounts. It is the earnings figure that tells us more about the profitability of the company than the dividends. It is this figure minus the dividends that determine the ability of the company to finance future expansion out of retained profits and reduces its vulnerability to interest rate changes in the loanable funds market.

An analogous calculation to the gross yield could be made by simply substituting the earnings per share figure for the gross dividend and the result would be an earnings yield as a percentage of the acquisition price of the share. By formula, this would be equal to

$$\frac{\text{earnings per share} \times 100}{\text{price}}$$

However, the published ratio is the reciprocal of this and the 100 is omitted. The published ratio is the price earnings ratio and it is conventionally presented as a ratio and not converted to a percentage. It is to this ratio that we now turn.

The price earnings ratio

A commonly reported statistic in the financial press is the ratio of the current price of the share to the last reported earnings per share on the net basis.

Example One

From the data quoted from the annual report of the Midland Bank for the year ended 31 December 1983, the quoted earnings per share of 60.60p may be divided into the price of the ordinary shares taken from the financial press on 21 March 1984 as 387p. Thus, the ratio is

$$\frac{\text{Price in p}}{\text{Earnings}} = \frac{387}{60.60} = 6.4$$
(net basis)

This figure agrees with reported P/E ratio in the *Financial Times* of 21 March. Indeed, the price and P/E data reported in the press is sufficient for the earnings per share on the net basis to be calculated. It is a simple example of three variables in one equation, any one can then be calculated if the other two are given.

Example Two
The ratio calcualted from annual account data for Cadbury Schweppes PLC is thus,

$$\frac{\text{Price in p}}{\text{Earnings}} = \frac{128}{13.60} = 9.41$$
$$\text{(net basis)}$$

Again, it is the ratio and the price that are commonly reported in the financial press but, as explained above, this enables the earnings per share to be calculated.

What is to be made of these two examples? What do they tell us about the respective merits of the two companies? Do they tell us anything about whether the Midland Bank Group shares are in any sense a better or worse buy than the shares of Cadbury Schweppes?

An average P/E ratio is published in the financial press. At the time to which these accounts relate, the average value was 13.4. Compared to this mean or average value, the P/E ratios of 6.4 for the Midland Bank Group and 9.4 for Cadbury Schweppes are both relatively low. These figures suggest that the market regards both of them as not growth stocks but rather as well-managed companies without the potential for above-average growth. By January 1987, the ratios had changed to 8.7 for the Midland Bank and 18.5 for Cadbury Schweppes against a market average of 14.6.

An interpretation of these changes would be along the following lines. In 1984, food and groceries as a sector represented by Cadbury Schweppes was regarded as having better growth prospects than banking represented by the Midland Bank. By January 1987, this was still the judgement of the market but the gap between the ratios had increased. Cadbury Schweppes was by then regarded as still more of a growth stock in comparison to the Midland Bank and to the market generally.

A P/E of 6.4 means that each 1p net profit attributable to the class of shares that we would acquire if we were to invest in the ordinary equity of the Midland Bank Group would cost us 6.4p. Each penny of such earnings in Cadbury Schweppes would cost us in this sense 9.4p, 47% more expensive than the earnings of the Midland Bank. This might suggest that the shares of the latter are a 'better buy' in some sense.

If buying shares means buying ownership of earnings, then is not 1p of earnings a homogeneous commodity in whatever company it is earned? Should we not therefore buy the 1p of earnings as cheaply as possible and therefore buy into those companies with the lowest possible P/E ratios we can find in the Stock Exchange listings? In this two-share example, it would mean selling Cadbury Schweppes shares and buying those of the Midland Bank Group.

It is certainly one consideration, but only one. If the previous paragraph contained sufficient criteria to guide investment portfolio planning, then P/E ratios would tend towards numerical equality. In our example, the price of Cadbury Schweppes shares would fall and those of the Midland Bank Group rise and thus, for given earnings, the two ratios would tend to converge.

An approximation to this is evident in the gilt market. It will be noticed that, for undated stocks, the price ratios are close to the coupon rate ratios. It should be apparent that the evaluation of an equity investment is vastly more complex than the evaluation of the respective merits of different coupon gilts.

A rise in the P/E ratio of an individual company may have nothing to do with changed views about the future prospects of the company itself but rather to do with changes in the general level of

Table 5.3 FT 30 Share Index annual highs and lows 1980–1983

Year	High	Low	Change
1980	515.9	406.9	× 1.27
1981	597.3	446.0	× 1.34
1982	637.4	518.4	× 1.23
1983	760.2	598.4	× 1.27

Source: 'Key Indicators World Bourses', *Economist*, 27.12.1980, 19.12.1981, 18.12.1982, 24.12.1983

stock market prices. It may be useful therefore, to compare changes in the P/E ratio to changes in the level of stock market prices generally by comparing the behaviour of the FT 30 Share Index (see Table 5.3) over a period of time. Changes in the P/E ratio 'out of line' with changes in the FT Index may then be attributed to factors relating to the company itself and not to changes in share prices generally. Note that this suggested comparison is not conclusive, it is only suggestive.

Thus, a change of 27% in a P/E ratio from an annual low to an annual high in 1980 may well have had more to do with stock market trends generally than with factors directly bearing on the company.

Another way of considering the same point is to compare the P/E ratio of an individual company to the published average figure for all quoted companies. The ups and downs of stock market price movements generally would leave the ratio of the P/E of one company to the average ratio of all companies unchanged. Any significant change in the ratio of these P/E ratios would then indicate factors that were of significance to the company itself and not to market conditions generally.

As P/E ratios of different companies do not tend to equality as suggested above that they would if the price of 1p of the last published earnings were the sole price-determining factor, other factors must be important in determining the relative P/E ratios.

Shares may be bought in the expectation of future earnings growth, hence in expectation of future increases in price and a mixed expectation of capital gains and dividend growth.

Expected future earnings may be thought sufficiently promising to justify a 'high' price now. Buy into the company now and, although the price appears high in relationship to current earnings, the present price may appear rather lower in the future if our judgement about the company's growth prospects is proved correct. Sometimes, considerations of this nature may produce very high P/E ratios of over 300. Certainly, P/E ratios of well over 50 are not uncommon in the more speculative stocks, particularly those quoted on the Unlisted Securities Market and the even more speculative Over the Counter Market.

In view of the previous paragraph, is it reasonable to regard relatively high P/E ratios as indicating growth potential shares? It may be, but the investor is cautioned to realise that there is never a guarantee of future growth. A 'high' P/E ratio is a market evaluation of the likely prospects of the company, not a flashing light showing a sure and certain route to capital gains.

The reader is invited to compare the P/E ratios for companies that have a full Stock Exchange listing to those quoted on the Over the Counter Market. The former have generally been established long enough for any rapid growth potential to have either been realised and the company to have settled down into perhaps some steady-state growth rate or to have been fully discounted in the present price of the share. The latter are relative newcomers with products often untried and not market-proven. The estimated market potential often then contains a large margin of guesswork, hope and anticipation. Thus, very high P/E ratios of this anticipatory nature are more often found in the OTC Market. For example, on 26 September 1983, The London Private Health Co's P/E ratio was 145.0 and 162.5 for the Microfocus Co. Such figures are way in excess of the Stock Market average of around 13 and much higher than those of long-established companies with a record of several years of established earnings. In such examples as have been quoted above from the OTC Market, such high P/E ratios do reflect anticipated future earnings. The realisation of such anticipated earnings often depends upon marketing untried market-untested services or products. A high P/E ratio may then signal a high degree of risk.

As an indication of how little guidance there often is about the future in a P/E ratio, consider the fortunes of the London and Liverpool Trust PLC and Polly Peck (Holdings) PLC.

Consider first the London and Liverpool Trust PLC. There was a rapid growth in earnings per share from 0.97p in 1980 to 7.5p in 1982. The fall in the P/E ratio from 39.18 in 1980 to 13.4 in 1981 was mainly due to a growth in the earnings per share compared to a much smaller rise in the share price. Another substantial rise in earnings per share by 1982 was accompanied by an even sharper rise in the share price, carrying the P/E to 54.67. A possible interpretation of this behaviour is that an initially high P/E was the result of a market valuation of this company's shares as a growth stock. Realised substantial growth in EPS led to an upwards evaluation of the future growth prospects and a further substantial rise in the P/E ratio derived from a substantial rise in the share price. Should we have accepted this market evaluation and bought the stock? The answer in fact is given on p. 000.

Consider next the behaviour of these ratios for Polly Peck (Holdings) PLC. The P/E ratio for these shares varied in 1983 from 24.86 to 6.2. Why? The growth prospects of the stock had been reappraised by the market. This was due to the dramatic fall in the share price already mentioned in the discussion above.

The point to remember is that judgements can be very volatile. They are not once formed, fixed for all time. They can and do alter very rapidly with the 'new view' being reflected in a revised P/E ratio.

It should be noted that earnings per share can be calculated either on a historic cost basis or a current cost basis. The historic cost accounting (HCA) makes no allowance for inflation whereas the current cost accounting (CCA) is an attempt to allow for the distorting effects of inflation in company accounting procedures.

Prior to 1981, the only procedure allowed was to calculate earnings per share on a historic cost basis. The dangers of such a procedure in a period of inflation may be simply illustrated.

Costs of production amounting to £100 are incurred in producing and bringing to market goods that produce a cash flow of £150. There is thus a profit of £50, out of which taxation and dividends would normally be paid. Suppose, because of inflation, that the cost of replacing the raw material used in the production process had risen to say £130 and the other associated costs had risen to make a new total cost of production of £150. The profit on a current cost basis would now be zero.

Using a historic cost basis of assessment of costs and revenues in a period of rapid inflation such as was experienced in the UK in the mid-1970s could well mean that many companies were actually paying taxes on losses in real terms.

Recognition of this as a problem reflected the experience of historically high inflation rates and the inevitable time lag before accounting procedures were allowed to adapt to the problems of allowing for the effects of inflation in a company's accounts meant that it was 1981 before the distinction between historic cost accounting and current cost accounting appeared in the presentation of a company's trading results.

Figures for the key statistics used to measure a company's performance are now presented normally in both HCA and CCA. The CCA estimates of earnings per share will obviously be lower than on the HCA basis in a period of inflation. If the general price level were to actually fall, the affect would be, of course, that the CCA values would be higher.

Cover

The idea of cover is essentially quite simple. If my income is £100 per week and I spend £50, then my expenditure is covered twice by my income. The cover ratio in this example is 2. This is essentially the notion in the published cover ratio. In the published data, the question answered by the cover ratio figure is how many times the dividend paid is covered by the earnings per share. The higher the cover figure, the smaller the proportion of earnings per share that is being distributed as dividends and hence the greater the proportion that is being retained within the company. Thus:

$$\text{Dividend cover} = \frac{\text{Earnings per share}}{\text{Dividend per ordinary share}}$$

For Cadbury Schweppes PLC, the earnings per share for the year ended 31 December 1983 were 13.60p on the net basis required by accounting practice and to satisfy the Stock Exchange listing requirements. The cover ratio is then calculated by dividing the dividend paid of 5.40p per ordinary share in these earnings to produce a ratio of 2.52. For the Midland Bank Group for the same accounting period, the Cover Ratio is 60.6p/ 25.5p = 2.38.

Note that these calculated cover ratios of 2.52 and 2.38 exceed the ratio values of 1.9 and 2.1 respectively printed for these companies in the *Financial Times* of 21 March 1984. Why the differences?

The differences arise because the *Financial Times* printed ratios are based on a figure for earnings per share calculated on the maximum distribution basis. As the discussion in the first part of the chapter has made clear, this method of calculating earnings produces a figure less than that derived from the net basis of calculation. This arises because the tax deduction is normally greater under the MDB basis than the net basis. Thus, the numerators in the ratio calculation are smaller than those using EPS taken from the annual accounts and report to shareholders.

The reader may well feel that cover ratios should be calculated with earnings estimated on the net basis of calcualtion. This basis

Table 5.4 Cover ratio calculations

Company	From the annual accounts for the year ended 31 December 1983		Calculated cover ratios = earnings per share/dividend	Cover ratios directly from the financial press[b]	Earnings per share implied by cover ratios in the previous column
	Earnings per share[a]	Dividend			
Cadbury Schweppes PLC	13.60p	5.40p	2.52	1.9	10.26
Midland Bank	60.60p	25.50p	2.38	2.1	53.55

[a] The earnings per share shown in the annual accounts are calculated on the net basis, i.e. assuming the actual dividend policy adopted by the company in that financial year. It yields a high earnings per share and hence a higher cover ratio than the earnings per share calculated on a maximum distribution basis which is used as the basis for the calculations reported in the financial press.

[b] As the cover ratios published in the financial press assume earnings calculated on a maximum distribution basis, the ratios and the dividend per share, both of which are routinely published, may be used to calculate the earnings per share on the MDB

[c] Net of tax at the standard rate. This was 30% for the period to which these accounts relate. It was reduced to 29% in the 1986 Budget

assumes that the appropriate value of earnings on which to base a cover ratio calculation is the level of earnings with the taxation deducted reflecting the dividend policy actually adopted, that is, the net basis of earnings calculation.

This discussion is summarised in Table 5.4. Although a perfectly meaningful cover ratio may be calculated using earnings estimated on the net basis, it is important to realise that this is not the basis used in the calculations reported in the financial press. Reported cover ratios are generally lower than they would be if the net basis for earnings were assumed, and thus suggest that a greater propor- tion of earnings were distributed as dividends than is actually the case.

Clearly, numerically, the cover ratio may be less than or greater than one.

Cover ratio > 1

In this case, the earnings per share are greater than the net dividend per ordinary share paid out. Thus, the company has retained earnings that are not distributed as dividends. Presumably, this will enable the company to finance any capital expansion programme out of its own resources than otherwise would be the case.

In the case of the Midland Bank Group, the cover ratio of $60.6/25.5 = 2.37$ tells us that only a fraction of the EPS has been distributed as a dividend payment. Specifically, the reciprocal of the cover ratio, $1/2.37 = 0.42$ tells us that 42% of the EPS has been distributed and that 58% has therefore been retained within the company.

Notice that we cannot use the printed cover ratios in this way if they are based on the calculation of EPS on the maximum distrib- ution basis. The ratios printed on this latter assumption are much more conservative estimates and serve the need of a common basis for inter-company comparisons and not the analysis of one com- pany's performance where we need calculations based on the actual taxation paid by the economy.

A very high cover ratio would indicate that a relatively low percentage of earnings was distributed as dividend payments. If continued over a period of years, this is one of the factors that may depress the share price and make the company the object of a takeover bid.

Cover ratio < 1

In this case, the earnings per share are less than the dividend per ordinary share paid out. Thus, the dividend is being paid out of reserves in part as well as from current earnings. The lower the numerical value of the ratio below 1, the more is being paid out as dividend from reserves, thus depleting the cash position of the company and reducing its ability to supply finance either for working capital purposes or for fixed capital formation out of its own resources.

Logically, one can imagine cover ratios of zero or less than zero. This would simply mean that the company was paying dividends when it was just breaking even with zero earnings per share, or making losses so that earnings per share were negative and dividends were being paid out of past profits in the form of a depletion of reserves. Thus, a zero or negative cover ratio would have a perfectly sensible meaning.

Movements in Stock Market prices–random walk theory

Some of the factors responsible for determining the prices of individual shares have been referred to in the discussion on ratios above. Prices are also determined by factors present in the economy generally and not specific to any one company. We may then ask if these other factors operate in any systematic way that might imply successful forecasting as a possibility.

If the stock market indices discussed in this book are plotted and the resultant time series examined, they typically look like the 'representative' graph of Figure 5.1.

There appears to be regularity in the peaks and troughs. Bull markets are followed by bear markets and turning points occur. All this suggests that forecasting is possible. To identify a direction of movement and to label it a trend is to suggest that factors are systematically at work over time to produce that trend. Identify the systematic factors, express them in a mathematical relationship to produce the existing terms in the series and then extrapolate to make our forecasts of as yet future values of the index.[12]

The graph of Figure 5.1 is drawn for a period embracing two marked upward or bull market trends and two downward or bear market movements. The straight lines *A* and *C* denote downward

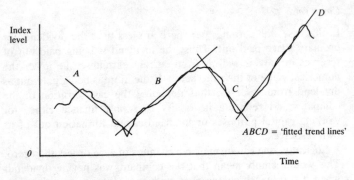

Figure 5.1   Representative graph of 'stock market trends'

trends and *B* and *D* upward trends. As soon as we do this as a means of summarising the overall movement for a period, we have imposed an interpretation on the data that may simply not reflect any underlying systematic set of determining forces at work. The appearance of a trend may be produced by a purely random generating mechanism. The series may 'walk' in a randomly generated fashion yet produce what looks like a trend.

To illustrate this, consider a coin-tossing experiment. Here the outcome of a toss of the coin is not influenced by any previous toss nor does it determine what the result will be of any future toss. Thus, knowledge of the results of a sequence of tosses to date does not enable the future sequence of the series to be forecast. The relevance of this to determining future share prices should be obvious.

To illustrate, a coin was tossed 52 times and the results recorded as follows:

HHHTTTHHTTTTTHHHHTTHTTTHHHTTTTTHHTTTTTTTHH-
HHHTTTHTTHHTT, that is, 23 heads and 29 tails. These results may be converted into a numerical score and graphed, assigning a head the score of +1 and a tail −1, as in Figure 5.2.

The graph drawn from the results of the coin-tossing experiment looks very much like a series of stock market index values over a period of time. There is the appearance of a trend: a minor bear market caused by the seven consecutive 'tails'. Had we assigned the

Cumulative
'score'

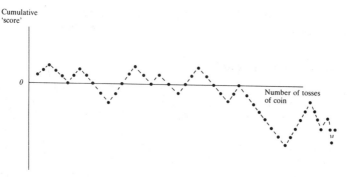

Figure 5.2   Results of coin tossing experiment

number -1 to a head and +1 to a tail, then the graph would have given the impression of a bullish trend, albeit a minor one.

It is the observation that the behaviour over time of stock market indices can be mimicked closely by coin-tossing experiments that leads many statisticians to regard the determination of stock market prices as essentially a random process or a random walk.[13] Random wander may be more appropriate a term.

The coin-tossing series shows apparent trends. Random wander theorists would see this as an interpretation imposed on the data after observing a series of unrelated values of what is essentially a random process.

The appearance of 'trends' is perfectly consistent with the random generating mechanism. It is similar to a random generator of numbered bingo balls producing a trend in say the run of 'odd' or 'even' numbers. Yet another example. The sex of children may be produced by a random process with probability of a boy or girl both equal to 0.5. Yet, even if this mechanism is random, it will still produce trends or runs in the sense of some large families of all boys or all girls.

Some identification of a trend from a randomly generated process is virtually certain for a small finite number of terms. This arises because we are unlikely to end a small finite series exactly where we started. Consider the uncertain path of a drunk in relation to a straight line. Though he starts to weave his uncertain path on the line, he will typically end some distance from the line. We would not want to use this 'trend' to forecast where he will head next!

Autocorrelated first differences

This section is a more technical discussion of what has been summarised above. Consider the behaviour of the FT 30 Share Index, term by term from 8 August 1984 to 24 October 1984. The series of closing values on a daily basis is listed in Table 5.5, along with the first difference terms of the series. The meaning of the term 'first differences' should be clear from the table.

We wish to examine this series to see whether the first differences of the series move in a systematic related way or whether they move in essentially a random uncorrelated way. In the first case, forecasting is possible whereas, in the latter case, the random walk or wander theory is supported and no forecasting is really possible.

This examination of the first differences of the series to see whether or not they move in a systematic related or correlated way can either be done in an impressionistic way by just looking and thinking about what the series suggests or we may calculate the numerical value of the correlation coefficient that measures the degree of autocorrelation in the series of first differences, that is, the extent to which the first differences move in a systematic related way or not.

The reader is invited to consider the series of first differences of the series–the pattern of changes in the index level from one closing level to the next. Is there anything that would lead him to confidently forecast the next values in the series from the information provided by the series of first differences to date?

Statistically, information about the randomness of the relationship between the first differences is measured by the calculation of the Pearson product-moment correlation coefficient. For details of this calculation, the reader is referred to any elementary statistics textbook.[14]

The correlation coefficient for the series of first differences given in Table 5.5 is 0.018. This relatively low value for the coefficient is supportive of the random walk hypothesis. The relationship between the numerical value of the coefficient and the implied forecastability of future values of the time series is summarised in Table 5.6.

Table 5.5 The FT 30 Share Index from 8 August to 24 October 1984

Closing value of the index	First differences	Closing value of the index	First differences
839.0	−11.9	859.0	− 1.0
827.1	+19.2	858.0	+13.8
846.3	− 5.8	871.8	− 3.6
840.5	+ 9.1	868.2	+ 3.2
849.6	− 8.0	871.4	− 8.0
841.6	− 7.5	863.4	+ 6.6
834.1	+ 4.2	870.0	− 1.0
838.3	− 5.1	869.0	+ 3.0
833.2	+ 6.7	872.0	− 3.6
839.9	+ 1.7	868.4	−11.5
841.6	− 6.4	856.9	+ 1.7
835.2	+ 1.6.	858.6	− 4.2
836.8	− 4.4	854.4	+ 3.4
832.4	+ 17.4	857.8	+ 5.4
849.8	+ 2.7	863.2	+ 3.4
852.5	+ 1.2	866.6	− 0.4
853.7	+ 1.4	866.2	+ 0.6
855.1	−16.8	866.8	+ 3.8
838.3	+ 1.6	870.6	− 0.6
839.9	+ 9.0	876.0	+ 5.6
848.9	+ 2.8	881.6	−15.2
851.7	− 4.3	866.6	−27.9
847.4	+10.6	838.7	− 4.2
858.0	− 0.4	834.5	+19.0
857.6	+ 1.2	853.5	+12.2
858.8	+ 0.6	867.7	− 1.5
859.4	− 0.4	866.2	

The data strongly supports the random walk hypothesis. The correlation coefficient of 0.018 is not significantly different from zero at the 1% level of significance ($t = 0.1299$). Therefore, the null hypothesis cannot be rejected. There is thus no information in the series that would enable us with any confidence to forecast the future terms in the series.

Consider the consequences of finding support in the data for the

Table 5.6 Forecasting

Correlation of first differences coefffiicient values		Comment
+1		Perfect forecasting on a rising 'bull' market
↓ Decreasingly accurate forecasts	Increasingly accurate forecasts ↑	No forecasting possible. No relationship exists between the first differences. Historical data gives no indication of the future values.
0		
↑ Decreasingly accurate forecasts	Increasingly accurate forecasts ↓	
−1		Perfect forecasting on a falling market.

random walk theory for the 'gambling contracts' discussed on pp. 000–00.

The index is as likely to fall as rise. Therefore, one would expect as many 'unsuccessful bets' in one direction as 'successful bets'. Given that, for a large number of punters the average amount staked on successful bets will equal the amount unsuccessfully staked, and that winning bets win less than losing bets lose for a given movement of the index, the random walk nature of the index shifts the financial advantage to the sellers of such contracts.

The random walk behaviour of stock market indices is not a new observation. It was observed and analysed earlier this century by Bachelier and Kendall.[15]

It means that there are no systematic factors consistently at work and thus that forecasting has to give way to pure guesswork about the future course of such indices. Placing money on the future course of such indices is thus akin to pure gambling despite the common belief otherwise.

One cannot, of course, prove a negative, that is, that there are no time series on Stock Market prices that exhibit or ever will exhibit a high degree of autocorrelation of first differences. What can be said is that a common characteristic of such price series that have been investigated is that they show relatively little, if any, autocorrelated first difference terms, that is, they conform very closely to the behaviour expected on an assumption of the random walk or random wander theory.

Individual share prices

The trends of Stock Market indices have been considered in terms of the random walk theory. What about trends in the prices of individual shares.[16]

They can be tested as above for properties akin to a random walk series and appear to conform to this principle. The essence of a random walk is that forecasting is dependent upon a relatively high degree of autocorrelated first differences and this is absent from a randomly moving series. Investigation of such time series typically shows a low coefficient of autocorrelation and thus forecasting is not really likely to be very successful.

Financial markets, on this view, are said to be weakly efficient, by which is meant that there is little or no relevant information in the historical series to forecast future values. This is typically the conclusion of the financial economist.

There are, however, general points that can be made about the behaviour of individual share prices. Typically, the range between the annual high and low price is found to be greater than the year-to-year variation in the high-to-high or low-to-low price. This means that capital appreciation is typically more dependent on when shares are bought and sold during the year than the period of time for which the shares are held.

Functions of stock markets

The markets for shares in the UK perform two main vital functions, the raising of finance for capital investment or for the privatisation of a nationalised industry by a new issue of shares, and also provide a market for the buying and selling of the ownership of existing capital.

As far as the second function is concerned, the market functions efficiently in the technical sense that the price moves to ensure that normally buyers are willing to buy the shares that sellers with to sell.

Although such prices movements are not forecastable with any degree of accuracy, they move so as to efficiently achieve their prime function of ensuring a market for listed shares.

This is an essential function of the markets' price mechanism. It ensures that subscribers to a company's capital can get the market value of their shares at any time. The liquidity[17] of such investments coupled to the provision of limited liability[18] means that industry is able to raise much larger sums of finance than would otherwise be possible.

The lack of price forecasting inherent in the way stock market prices move is a problem when deciding upon the price to attach to a new issue of shares. This problem has been highlighted by the publicity attached to the extensive privatisation policy[19] of Conservative governments since 1979.

Privatisation and share prices

Privatisation, or the denationalisation of state-owned industries, has been a major policy of the Conservative governments elected since 1979.[20] This section does not concern itself with the general problems and arguments for and against privatisation but with the problem of deciding the price at which the shares are to be sold that will achieve the transfer of the resources from the public to the private sector.

One of the fundamental technical problems of privatisation is the setting of the offer price for the shares, given that the aim is to set a price that will not be 'too low' in that the issue is heavily oversubscribed nor 'too high' in that the issuers are left with an undersubscribed issue.[21]

The general problem is illustrated by Figure 5.3. To ensure that a new issue of shares is neither underscribed (by $x_2 - x_1$ at a price of 160p) nor oversubscribed (by $x_3 - x_2$ at a price of 130p) is to try to shoot at a moving point, the initial position of which and the velocity of displacement of which are at best clouded in uncertainty and sometimes completely unknown.

The diagram summarises generally the market situation relating to any new issue, whether the aim is to privatise a nationalised industry or to raise finance for the capital expansion programme of a public limited liability company. The vertical line at x_2 equals the number of shares to be issued–the supply curve of economic theory.

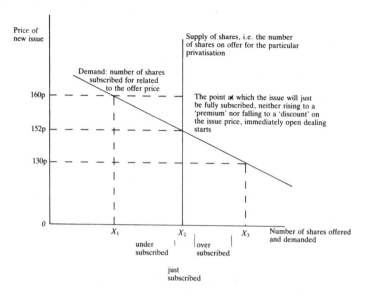

Figure 5.3 New issue market for share issue to raise capital for investment or for a 'privatisation' issue

Once the size of the issue to be made has been determined, the position of x_2 is uniquely determined. The demand curve $D–D$ shows the usually assumed negatively sloped relationship between the demand for the share as a function of its price. Our diagram shows one price, 152p per share in the diagram, at which the issue is just subscribed. The difficulty is that this demand curve is constantly shifting as factors altering the attractiveness of the shares at any given themselves change. The reader is invited to more realistically view the demand curve, not so much as a fixed line, but a blur as it shifts more or less constantly. Even if the curve's position were exactly known at the point in time at which the offer price was set, then it may well have shifted before the investing public has made its response to the terms and conditions set out in the prospectus accompanying the offer for sale.

The extent of apparent oversubscription is no guide either to the distance $x_3 - x_2$. Multiple applications for shares may be made to

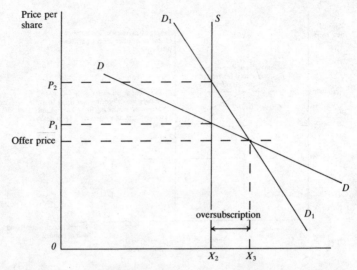

Figure 5.4 Relationship between share price and the demand curve given a particular degree of oversubscription

ensure the number actually obtained if the bids are 'scaled down' corresponds more closely to the number actually demanded at the issue price.

The extent of the premium to which the share price rises when open trading takes place is also little guide to the extent of oversubscription. Consider Figure 5.4.

A given level of oversubscription may be associated with an offer price that is only marginally below what would be the equilibrium price, or with a price that is way below the true equilibrium price, that is, the price at which the issue would just have been subscribed. The premium created by the impact of the unsatisfied demand for the share at its offer price is shown to be dependent on the price elasticity of demand for the shares. The given oversubscription, $x_3 - x_2$, is associated with a price rise from the offer price to $P1$, given the demand curve, $D–D$, and with the much higher price $P2$, given the relatively more price-inelastic demand curve, $D1–D1$.

An oversubscribed issue means that a larger amount of finance could have been raised by the sale of the same number of shares at the higher price suggested by the amount of the opening premium. This is of course hindsight. A higher price would have meant a greater risk of the issue being undersubscribed. This would have meant, in the absence of the issue being underwritten,[22] that insufficient finance had been raised to meet the privatisation target.

It is in bidding for shares in the hope that the issue will be oversubscribed and that consequently the price will rise to a premium over the issue price that the 'stag' finds his profit.[23] In this respect, the 1984 privatisation of the Jaguar Motor Co. PLC at an offer price of 165p per share was a disappointment to the stags only rising to a premium of around 15p per share whereas the £4,000,000,000 privatisation of British Telecom the same year at 130p per share led to initial premiums of around 45p[24] on the initial partly paid price of 50p, a premium of some 90%.

The beta coefficient

There is one area in which analysts claim to have found systematic behaviour in individual share prices. During periods of generally rising Stock Market prices, the price of an individual share may typically move up by more or less than the average. This is inevitably so in one sense because an average level is itself an average of individual values, some of which will rise by more and others by less than the average. The interesting question for investors is of course whether or not typically the same shares rise by more or less as the general level changes.

The stock market indices considered are in the nature of averages. It follows from the nature of an average that, if the average is rising, then some individual share prices will be rising faster and some more slowly than the average.

An average rise of 10% might be the result of share X rising by 20% and share Y by 5%. Thus, the ß coefficients are calculated as follows:

$$\beta_x = \frac{\text{Change in the price of share x}}{\text{Change in the index}} = \frac{20\%}{10\%} = 2$$

$$ß_y = \frac{\text{Change in the price of share y}}{\text{Change in the index}} = \frac{5\%}{10\%} = 0.5$$

The coefficient is simply the ratio of the change in the price of a share related to the change in the overall index at the same time. Shares with high ßs are the ones to hold during a bull market and the ones to avoid if a bear market is expected. Low ßs are to be preferred if the index is expected to fall. Negative ßs would be attractive in conditions of a falling market and to be avoided in a rising market.

Some of the problems in making use of such coefficients are obvious. Given the ßs, the direction of movement of the index has to be assumed when using this data in portfolio selection. The random walk theory discussed above gives us no reason for confidence that this is possible.

Then, there is the nature of the coefficient itself. How stable are these ßs over time as the individual share price and the index change over time? These are questions that have been the subject of some research, and ß calculations are now made available commercially.[25]

Notes

1. *Statements of Standard Accounting Practice*, August 1974, M3, P. 3. The Institution of Chartered Accountants in England and Wales.
2. The method discussed for calculating the denominator is outlined in the reference noted in Note 1.
3. Reduced to 29% in the 1986 Budget.
4. 71/29 from the 1986 Budget.
5. The gross dividend payment of the Midland Bank for the year ended 31 December 1983 is 36.4p. This figure is obtained by 'grossing up' at the standard rate of income tax of 30%. 30% of this is thus 10.9p and is the ACT payment and 70% or 25.5p is the net dividend. These figures satisfy the 70/30 rule. Similarly for Cadbury Schweppes, the gross dividend is 7.7p for the same accounting period. 30% of this is 2.3p and is thus the ACT payment and 5.4p the net dividend. These figures satisfy the 70/30 rule.
6. It may be carried forward for a maximum of 2 years and offsetted against MCT.

7   J. A. Kay, and M. A. King, *The British Tax System*, p. 185, Oxford University Press, 1983.

8   Following the budgetary changes of April 1986, the reduction of the standard rate of income tax from 30% to 29% would of course increase the net dividend for a given gross payment. The gross payment may be affected by the tax rate reduction depending upon how, if at all, this affects the company's deliberations about its dividend policy.

9   Following the reduction in the standard rate of tax in April 1986 to 29%, the multiplier in subsequent calculations would of course be 100/71.

10 With the exception of index-linked stocks as discussed above.

11 See articles in the *Investors' Chronicle*, Vol. 68, 24 February and 27 April 1984: 'Bare essentials' and 'Dilution threat'.

12 The reader interested in the technical problems of fitting trend lines to such data is referred to any statistics textbook dealing with the least squares method of estimating 'regression lines'.

13 S. S. Alexander, 'Price movements in speculative markets: trends or random walks', *Industrial Management Review*, Vol. 12, No. 2, May 1961, pp. 7–26.

14 For example, M. J. Moroney, *Facts from Figures*, p. 422, Penguin, Harmondsworth.

15 Louis Bachelier, *Theory of Speculation*, Paris, 1900. M. G. Kendall, 'The analysis of economic time series Pt. I Prices', *Journal of the Royal Statistical Society*, Vol. 96, Pt. I, 1953, pp. 11–25. Both are reprinted in P. H. Cootner, (ed.) *The Random Character of Stock Market Prices*, MIT Press, Cambridge, Mass., 1964.

16 See, for example, the price date series on each Stock Exchange listed share published by the Extel Statistical Services Ltd.: the *Extel Cards*.

17 The ease with which an investment can be turned into cash.

18 Liability for the debts of the economy only extending to the investment itself and not to the full extent of his assets.

19 The denationalising of a state-owned industry by the sale of shares by an offer for sale at a predetermined price.

20 At the time of writing in January 1987, the privatised industries include British Aerospace, British Petroleum, Cable and Wireless, Amersham International, Britoil, Associated British Ports, Enterprise Oil, Jaguar Motor Company, Trustee Savings Bank, British Telecom and British Airways.

21 For a survey of the financial consequences of a portfolio of investments in privatisation issues, see 'Spectrum', *The Times*, 23 April 1986, p. 14.

22 It is normal for the issue organisers, often a merchant bank, to underwrite or agree to take up any shares not sold in response to the issue of the offer in the privatisation prospectus.

23 A stag buys shares in a new issue in the hope of quickly being able to resell at a profit. The origin of the term is uncertain but it is said to have originated from the queuing that took place in Stag Lane London to await new issues.

24 The word 'around' is used advisedly. Trading took place both on the Stock Market and in the so-called Grey Market away from the floor of the Stock Exchange itself, leading to some variations in the actual premium levels reached.

25 Coefficients are calculated and published by the London Business School.

Chapter Six

The London Traded Share Options Market

The London Traded Share Options Market dates from 1978. Its stock-in-trade is the purchase and sale of options to buy or sell shares.

A may agree, in return for consideration paid now, to sell to B the option, exercisable at B's behest, to require A to purchase from or sell to him, just about anything at any point of time during say the next 3 months at a price agreed now. The option becomes a traded option if the option is a negotiable instrument and hence if A may sell this option to C. For example, I could sell you the option for say £10 to buy my car for £1,000 between now and 3 months hence. The effective price of you acquiring the car would then be £1,010, that is, exercise price plus premium.

The motor car illustration is of an option contract that would be purely a private arrangement between one buyer and one seller. The option premium or price would be negotiated solely between the buyer and seller and any risk would be solely between the two parties to the contract. The option terms would be peculiar to the one contract and in no sense could a market be said to exist: it would only be a one-off bargain between two people.

For an organised market to exist and develop, standardised contracts are required. At present in the UK, option contracts are traded on some 24 shares of leading companies. The initial life of the option is for 3.6 or 9 months. The contracts are so arranged that it is possible to buy or sell options expiring in any month of the year.

On 4 May 1984 there were some 4,433 contracts concluded on the Traded Options Market. Some 70% of these were call options–the options that enables buyers to acquire shares at a particular exercise price. For example, a BP July 390 Call Option at 133 means that the buyer of such an option between 4 May and the expiry of the option in July may call upon the writer or supplier of the option to sell to him British Petroleum Co. shares at a strike price of 390p each in return for a premium paid now of 133p per share. Acquiring shares in this way would mean an effective acquisition price of 523p each–the sum of the premium and strike price. The other 30% of contracts are put options–the option that the buyer acquires to require the writer to buy shares from him at an agreed price. For example, a BP 390 July put option at 3p. In return for receiving a premium now of 3p per share, the option writer stands ready to buy BP shares at a price of 390p per share between 4 May and the expiry of the option in July 1984.

In a traded option market, therefore, prices are publicly quoted and are determined by the forces of supply and demand, with numerous buyers and sellers. A secondary market exists in which the option itself can be traded. Indeed, this facility is a large part of the *raison d'être* of the traded options market, being the source of major profit opportunities.

For such an organised wide market to exist, as discussed above, standardised option terms have to exist as a necessary condition for an offered market. This means, in particular, a finite small number of maturity dates and a relatively small number of shares.

Although individual writers supply the options and individuals buy them, there is a clearing-house arrangement guaranteeing performance of the contract. In the case of the UK Traded Options Market, this is the London Options Clearing House organised and supervised by the London Stock Exchange.

The put option

A put option is, in this example, the option of selling a particular share at a given price (the option exercise or strike price) during the life of the option. For example, a July 550 Put Option could be purchased for 3p per share on 1 May 1984. This would entitle the buyer, at his option, to require the seller of the option to buy ICI shares from him at a price of 550p per share between 1 May and the expiry of the option in July 1984 irrespective of the open market price for ICI shares.

As such an option was traded at 3p per share, the likelihood of the option being exercised was regarded as being rather slight, that is, a low probability was assigned to the possibility of it being exercised.

It is easy to see why this should be so. The underlying share could be sold for 628p on 1 May 1984. Only if the underlying share price were to fall below 550p during the life of the option would it be worthwhile exercising the option. No one would be likely to exercise an option to sell if the shares could be sold at a higher price on the Stock Exchange. Thus, put options are a way of betting on a bear market in the shares of a particular company for a known maximum loss equal to the premium paid as far as the buyer is concerned. It is also a way of hedging against a fall in share prices. If a portfolio is to be sold at a future date, buying put options is a way of 'locking in' to the prices prevailing today.

The buyer of a Put Option needs to be right about the direction of anticipated price changes, the amount of the change and the timing of the change. Only if he gets all three correct, will profits be maximised from operations in the Traded Options Market.

Table 6.1 Traded option data: ICI Shares July 1984 put option

Option exercise price	Option prices (premiums)		% change in option premiums
	1.5.1984 USP 628p	5.5.1984 USP 602p	
(i) 550p	3p	5p	+67
(ii) 600p	13p	20p	+53.85
(iii) 650p	36p	52p	+44.44

% change in the price of the underlying share price (USP) = 4.14

(i,ii) On 1 May 1984, these option exercise prices are both less than the underlying share price, i.e. they have no *intrinsic value*, they are said to be *out of the money*

(iii) On 1 May 1984, this option is *in the money*, i.e. it has *intrinsic value* of 650p – 628p = 22p per share

Inspection of Table 6.1 shows a direct relationship between the option exercise price and the premium or price paid to acquire the option. In relationship to a given underlying share price, this is to be expected. The higher the option exercise price in relationship to the underlying share price, the more likely it is to be exercised and to be triggered by a smaller fall in the underlying share price. Thus the writer is able to demand and the buyer willing to pay a higher premium, their competing interests being mediated by market forces into a single equilibrium price for each option exercise price.

Further inspection of the table shows a sharp increase in premiums from 1 to 4 May, increases varying from 44% to 67% associated with a fall in the underlying security price from 628p to 602p.

A fall in the Underlying Share Price makes it more likely that the options will be exercised. The lower a share price falls, the more valuable an option to sell at a given price becomes. The principle is illustrated in Figure 6.1.

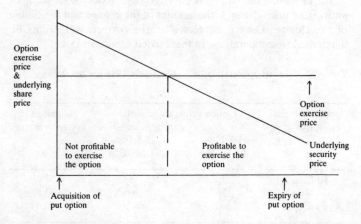

Figure 6.1 Relationship between the underlying security price and the option exercise price

The rise in option premiums over the 4 days from 1 to 5 May will be sharper the more the 4.14% fall in the underlying security price is interpreted by market opinion as the beginning of a sustained downward movement, and will be smaller the more the movement is thought to be a more or less random fluctuation in the price without much significance for any overall trend.

The relatively large changes in premiums over a period of a few

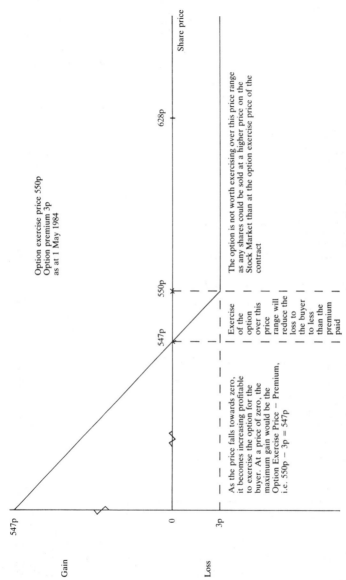

Option exercise price 550p
Option premium 3p
as at 1 May 1984

The option is not worth exercising over this price range as any shares could be sold at a higher price on the Stock Market than at the option exercise price of the contract

Exercise of the option over this price range will reduce the loss to the buyer to less than the premium paid

As the price falls towards zero, it becomes increasing profitable to exercise the option for the buyer. At a price of zero, the maximum gain would be the Option Exercise Price − Premium, i.e. 550p − 3p = 547p

Share price

628p

550p

547p

Gain

Loss

547p

0

3p

Figure 6.2 Traded option data: ICI shares July 1984 put option – position facing the buyer

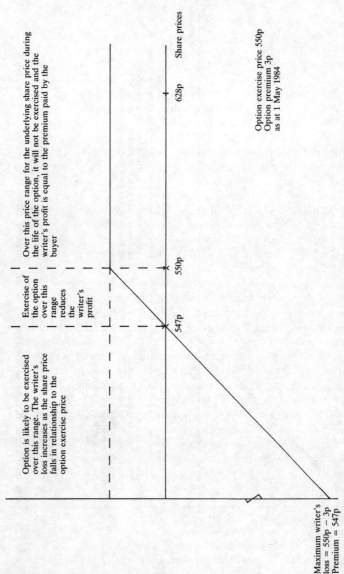

Over this price range for the underlying share price during the life of the option, it will not be exercised and the writer's profit is equal to the premium paid by the buyer

Share prices

Exercise of the option over this range reduces the writer's profit

Option is likely to be exercised over this range. The writer's loss increases as the share price falls in relationship to the option exercise price

628p

550p

547p

Option exercise price 550p
Option premium 3p
as at 1 May 1984

Maximum writer's
loss = 550p − 3p
Premium = 547p

Figure 6.3 Traded option data: ICI shares July 1984 put option – position facing the option writer

days shows the extent to which interest may focus on the *traded* nature of the option. Options are bought and sold to an extent, not simply to hedge the possibility of an adverse price movement in the underlying security but with the intention of making a profit from the trading and thus to be able to take advantage from a favourable movement in premiums.

There are two quite distinct ways of looking at these processes. Essentially, the behaviour of individual share prices and the general level of share prices during the life of an option is uncertain. One may form a view on the course of such prices and have a hunch held with more or less conviction, but accurate forecasts reflect luck rather than scientific accuracy and the application of convincing models of price determination.

One view is that buying and selling options is essentially gambling–playing a game of chance for money. From the point of view of the buyer, the stake is the premium paid. The 'winnings' are uncertain and cannot be known in advance. In the event of loss, the amount is limited to the stake, that is, the premium paid to acquire the option.

The second view is that we live in an uncertain world in which we cannot know how share prices and exchange rates will move over the next few weeks or months. Our asset position will strengthen or weaken depending upon whether the prices of securities we possess rise or fall. We can protect or hedge the risk of unfavourable movements by an appropriate option strategy. Viewed in this way, action in the traded options market is more akin to taking out insurance against other uncertainties than to gambling.

Table 6.1 shows the Put Option data from which Figures 6.2 and 6.3 are constructed showing the position faced by the buyer and the writer respectively of such an option.

The probability of a gain for the buyer and a loss to the writer close to the maximum possible of 547p is very low indeed. Remember, it would mean that ICI shares, currently at 628p on 1 May 1984, had fallen to virtually zero. What sort of disastrous scenario would this imply?

The figures indicate that the maximum loss for the buyer and the maximum profit for the writer are the same, and equal to the premium of 3p per share. The writer needs to balance the known certain relatively small premium income received against the probability of very much larger losses if the underlying share price moves down in relationship to the option exercise price sufficiently to trigger the exercise of the option. The writer does face a known maximum theoretical loss which will occur if the underlying share price falls to zero. This will be equal to the option exercise price less the premium received, a total of 547p per share in the particular example given.

Selling put options[1] is one way of possibly acquiring shares if the buyer chooses to exercise the option he has been sold. If the option writer feels the price is attractive, he will either acquire the shares if the option is exercised against him or simply receive the premium if the option is not exercised. ICI shares at 550p may be viewed as attractive purchases. For the option writer to acquire shares in this way is contingent upon the buyer choosing to exercise the option to sell to the writer: it cannot of course be triggered by the writer at his discretion, the option belongs to the buyer. The effective price of acquisition would be 447p per share–the Option Exercise Price minus the premium. If the option is not exercised, the writer has the premium. If it be exercised on a fall in the underlying share price to below 550p, the writer will have to acquire the shares at a price currently in excess of the market price (otherwise, the option would not have been exercised). This may not be that important so long as the writer has funds to acquire the shares and has formed the view that the shares are 'reasonably priced' in relationship to longer-run considerations of the company's position.

Acquiring shares in this way by writing a put option is a two-stage process. The first stage is the receipt of the premium. The second stage involves waiting for the buyer to decide on share price movements if he will exercise the option. It would be possible for the option writer to have his funds usefully invested on the money market during this period and only paid to the buyer on exercise of the option. Thus, the interest income may cover the loss on exercise of the option if the underlying share price is then just below the option exercise price and thus the option is just worth exercising from the point of view of the buyer.

Buying a July put option in say March fixes a price for a sale that will transfer a realised capital gain to the next tax year.[2] Why not simply wait until July and sell at the prevailing market price? The investor may want to 'lock in' to today's prices, fearing a decline in prices between March and July. If he is wrong and prices rise between these dates, he can then sell on the open market and either lose his premium or sell it for any time value it may still possess.

The call option

A call option is, in this example, the option of buying a particular share at a given exercise or strike price during the life of the option. For example, on 15 May 1984, payment of a price or premium of 103p would buy the option of acquiring British Petroleum shares between then and July 1984 by a further payment of 390p per share. Inspection of the data in Table 6.2 shows that this would mean a total purchase price by this two-stage process of 493p compared to the direct single transaction purchase at the underlying share price of 488p.

Table 6.2   Traded option data: BP shares July 1984 call option

Option exercise price (p)[c]	Option prices (premiums)[a]		% change in option premiums	Effective share acquisition price 15.5.1984[d]
	15.5.1984 USP = 488p	22.5.1984 USP = 538p[b]		
390	103	155	50.49%	493
420	73	125	71.23%	493
460	42	85	102.38%	502
500	17	45	164.71%	517
550	8	18	125.00%	550

[a]   The price of acquiring the option to purchase BP shares between the stated date and expiry of the option in July 1984
[b]   The underlying share price: the price of acquiring BP shares by direct purchase, e.g. 488p on 15.5.1984
[c]   The price to be paid to the option writer by the option buyer on exercising the option to acquire the shares
[d]   Effective share acquisition price: sum of the option exercise price and the option premium

Although this is 5p dearer than acquiring the shares by a single direct purchase, it does mean that only the 103p would be paid on 15 May 1984 and the 390p on exercising the option during the time between then and the expiry of the option contract in July of that year.

Using the Traded Options Market in this way to acquire shares enables the buyer to lock in to a price of 390p and not exercise the option until nearer the July expiry date. If the buyer of the option contract already has the cash, he can invest it on the Money Market at interest until he is ready to exercise the share purchase option. The availability of short-term lending facilities on the Money Market means that, in certain cases, the net cost of acquiring shares in this two-stage way may actually be a cheaper way of buying shares than by direct purchase in one transaction in the 'normal' way. It is also a means of setting a price of acquisition of the underlying shares now and exercising the option at a future date when an expected cash inflow occurs. Thus, we may be unable to purchase shares now because we do not have enough ready cash but expect it some time between now and the expiry of the option. The option allows us but does not compel us to acquire shares at today's prices and not at the uncertain cost of acquisition at some point of time in the future.

It is also a way of backing 'bullish' views about the future trend in the price of the underlying shares. A total price of acquisition (option premium plus exercise price) of 493p per share on 15 May 1984 compares to an underlying share price one week later of 538p and hence a capital gain of 45p, a 9.13% capital gain in one week. This assumes that the option is exercised at 390p per share and the shares then sold at the price of 538p.

It is important to remember that these contracts are not just option contracts exercisable at the option of the buyer but traded options. The option may be sold or traded by the initial buyer to a third party: the option contract is a negotiable instrument. Indeed, a major motive in buying an option is to subsequently sell the option itself, hopefully at a profit.

A characteristic of the Traded Options Market is the relationship displayed in Table 6.2 between changes in the price of the underlying share and changes in the option prices. Generally, a relatively low percentage change in the price of the underlying share triggers a relatively high percentage change in the related option premiums.

Inspection of the table shows that a 10.25% change in the BP share price during one week in May 1984 is associated with option premium changes ranging from 50.49% to 164.71%. For example, buyers of BP July 460 Call Option contracts on 15 May 1984 at 42p could have sold these a week later at a price of 85p, a 102.38% gain in 7 days. Thus, the traded nature of the option is a characteristic of these contracts that provides the opportunity for considerable profit in a short space of time. Of course, prices can move the other way. It should never be forgotten that coupled to a chance of a large gain is nearly always the possibility of equally large losses the other way. The probability of gain must always be balanced by a probability of loss if a market is to exist. It is a necessary condition for trade to take place, as is differing expectations of buyers and writer about which way, on a balance of probabilities, prices will move in the future.

Hindsight is of course a wonderful teacher as to what one's investment strategy should have been to maximise gain over a given period. A static comparison of prices at two points of time can also be misleading and lead one to seriously underestimate the dynamics of the Traded Options Market. It is a very fast-moving market and needs continuous monitoring if advantage is to be taken of any favourable price movements.

The summary data in Table 6.2 on activities in the Traded Options Market shows the expected inverse relationship between the option exercise price and the option premium. As the option exercise price rises, so the associated premium falls. It should be easy to see why this should be so. In the table, as the option exercise price rises from 390p to 550p, so the premium, the price of the option, falls from 103p to 8p per share. The higher the option exercise price for a call option in relationship to a given underlying share price, the lower the probability that the underlying share price will rise, during the life of the option contract, to a level at which it will be profitable to exercise the option. Competition in the Traded Options Market ensures that this results in the inverse relationship mentioned.

The option buyer and the option writer

Figure 6.4 summarises the position facing the writer of a call option and Figure 6.5 the position faced by the buyer of the same call option. The diagrams are mirror images of each other.

As may be seen by inspection of the diagrams, the maximum cost in this case to the buyer in Figure 6.4 of 103p per share is the

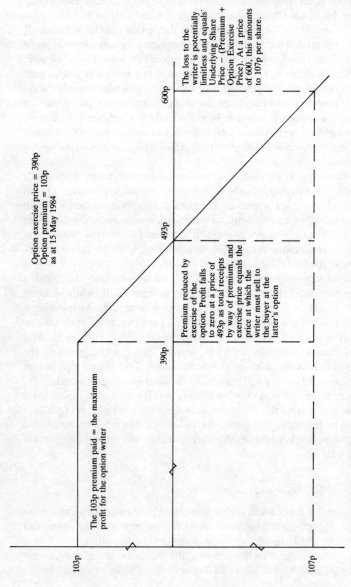

Option exercise price = 390p
Option premium = 103p
as at 15 May 1984

The 103p premium paid = the maximum profit for the option writer

Premium reduced by exercise of the option. Profit falls to zero at a price of 493p as total receipts by way of premium, and exercise price equals the price at which the writer must sell to the buyer at the latter's option

The loss to the writer is potentially limitless and equals' Underlying Share Price – (Premium + Option Exercise Price). At a price of 600, this amounts to 107p per share.

Figure 6.4 Traded option data: BP shares July 1984 call option – position facing the writer

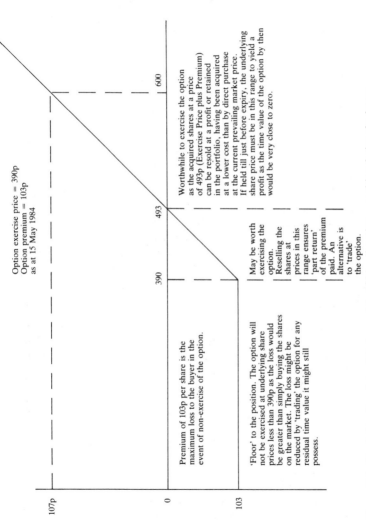

Option exercise price = 390p
Option premium = 103p
as at 15 May 1984

107p

0

103

390   493   600

Premium of 103p per share is the maximum loss to the buyer in the event of non-exercise of the option.

'Floor' to the position. The option will not be exercised at underlying share prices less than 390p as the loss would be greater than simply buying the shares on the market. The loss might be reduced by 'trading' the option for any residual time value it might still possess.

May be worth exercising the option. Reselling the shares at prices in this range ensures 'part return' of the premium paid. An alternative is to 'trade' the option.

Worthwhile to exercise the option as the acquired shares at a price of 493p (Exercise Price plus Premium) can be resold at a profit or retained in the portfolio, having been acquired at a lower cost than by direct purchase at the current prevailing market price. If held till just before expiry, the underlying share price must be in this range to yield a profit as the time value of the option by then would be very close to zero.

Figure 6.5 Traded option data: BP shares July 1984 call option – position facing the buyer

maximum profit for the option writer shown in Figure 6.5. This occurs in the case of non-exercise of the option and the holding of the option to expiry. The writer begins to lose, on exercise of the option, between a price of 390p and one of 493p. His loss between these prices is mirrored by the option buyer's gains over the same price range.

The buyer's potential gain is limitless, as is the writer's corresponding losses as share prices rise. In practice, share price rises are not infinite although sharp rises of considerable size can and do occur.

At an underlying price of 600p per share, the loss to the buyer, if the option is exercised, is 107p per share as is the buyer's gain.

The position is complicated slightly by the fact that the seller may be *naked* or *covered*. He is said to be naked if he does not possess the shares on which he has sold call options and covered if he does possess the underlying shares. The problem of selling call options if he is naked is obvious. If the option is exercised, he must then buy the shares at the prevailing market price. Thus, ignoring transaction costs,[3] the loss will be 107p per share. If he is covered, he may have acquired the shares at a considerably lower or higher price than the price he is now required to sell them for on exercise of the option by the buyer. He may wish to calculate his losses in relationship to these prices and hence arrive at a figure different from the 107p discussed above.

Intrinsic value

Table 6.3 shows variations in the *intrinsic value* of the July 1984 call options used as an illustrative example in this chapter. Arithmetically, the intrinsic value of each option is equal to the underlying share price minus the call option exercise price. Thus, if the share could currently be acquired by direct purchase on the Stock Exchange at a price of 488p and a call option at a price of 390p exists, then the intrinsic value is equal to 98p.

The concept of intrinsic value sometimes causes conceptual difficulty for the student of the Traded Options Market. Something that has intrinsic value has value inherent in itself. In this case, something that cost 488p on the Stock Market for immediate purchase could be bought by exercising an option to purchase at a lower exercise price of 390p. Thus, there is value inherent in or intrinsic to the option in that it enables shares to be acquired more

Table 6.3 Intrinsic value and time value: July 1984 Call options

Underlying share price BP shares 15.5.1984	Option exercise price	Intrinsic value	Comment
488p	390p	98p	These options are *In-the-money*, i.e. they are said to have *intrinsic value*
488p	420p	68p	
488p	460p	28p	
* 488p	(488p)	(0)	*At-the-money*, i.e. *zero intrinsic value*
488p	500p	−12p	These options are *Out-of-the-money*. They have arithmetically negative *intrinsic value*. Most writers regard them as for practical purposes zero *Intrinsic value*.
488p	550p	−62p	

Intrinsic value at a given date = Underlying share price − Call option exercise price.

* Included for completeness; there was no actual option traded at this price on 15 May 1984

cheaply than the current market price for direct purchase. In thinking about the concept of intrinsic value, forget for the moment that the option premium has to be added to the option exercise price to obtain the actual or effective purchase price of shares bought in this two-stage process via the initial acquisition of a call option on the shares.

Share options that have intrinsic value are also described as being *in the money*. Again, the meaning of this term is simply that the option exercise price is less than the underlying share price. The extent to which a share option is in the money or has intrinsic value is a value in pence equal to the difference between the underlying share price and the option exercise price.

From the above, and by inspection of Table 6.3, it should be clear what is meant by an option being *at the money* and having *zero intrinsic value*, and also options that are *out of the money* and have *negative intrinsic value*.

No option writer would sell a call option where the sum of the exercise price and the option premium together were less than the current underlying price of the share, so that an in-the-money option must await a rise in the price of the underlying share price before it is worth exercising. Do not confuse intrinsic value with the conditions that make it profitable to exercise an option.

Time value

The time value of an option is defined as the option premium minus the intrinsic value. An example is shown in Table 6.4. It will be observed that this quantity rises with the option exercise price. The greater the option exercise price, the more the underlying share price has to rise to justify the exercise of the option from the point of view of the buyer of the option. Thus are time value and the option exercise price linked. Having deducted the intrinsic value of an option from the option premium, we are left with an amount in pence per share that we have paid for our share option in excess of

Table 6.4   Time value: July 1984 call option BP shares

Underlying share price BP shares 15.5.1984 USP	Option exercise price OEP	Option premium OP	Intrinsic value = USP–OEP = IV	Time value OP–IV
488p	390p	103p	98	5p
488p	420p	73p	68	5p
488p	460p	42p	28	14p
(488p)	(488p)	(30p)	0	(30p)
488p	500p	17p	−12	29p
488p	550p	8p	−62	70p

Time value at a given date = option premium − intrinsic value

its intrinsic value. This amount is paid in the hope that the time we have between acquisition of the option and its expiry or subsequent resale will see the development take place that will justify the excess of the price paid over the intrinsic value. This is of course, for call options, that there will be such a bull market for the share in question that we can exercise the option profitably or sell it at a profit. The time-value element in the option price will of course decline towards zero as the expiry date of the option approaches.

Both the call and put options discussed above show sharp rises in premium over the periods covered. This may be misleading. The Call Option date on British Petroleum shares relates to a period in which the underlying share price was rising and the Put Option data on ICI shares to a period in which the underlying share price was falling. These are just the movements that make it more likely that the options may be exercised. Thus, the premiums rise. Had the price movements in the underlying share prices been in the other direction, the premiums would have fallen and option traders would have experienced sharp losses as a decreased liklihood of the options being exercised would have caused the associated premiums to fall. This is summarised in Table 6.5.

Table 6.5 Relationship between movements in the underlying share price and the option premium

Movement in the underlying share price	Effects on option premium	
	Call option	Put option
Rise	Rise (illustrated by the BP share example	Fall
Fall	Fall	Rise (illustrated by the ICI share example

Currency options

The traded options considered so far relate to hedging risks related to share price movements. Another increasingly important class of options relate to hedging the risks associated with exchange rate movements. Anyone involved with the purchase and sale of foreign currencies is at risk from the fluctuating relationship between currencies.

Examination of Table 6.6 shows an effective price of buying £1 via a June call option would have been 151c on 5 April 1984 as opposed to 144.65c on the spot market for virtual immediate direct purchase.[4] The effective price is the sum of the option strike price of 150c and the 1.00c premium paid to the writer of the option. The effective price is of course the total sum that has to be paid out by way of the price and premium as parts of the two-step process of acquisition.

In return for the 1.00c premium payable now, the buyer, as before, has acquired the right but not the obligation, to require the option writer to sell sterling to him as a price of £1 = 150c any time between acquisition of the option and its expiry date.

In return for a premium of 2.60c per £1, a put option buyer acquires the option to require the writer to buy pounds sterling from him at an exchange rate of 145c = £1 between option acquisition and the expiry date.

We live in an uncertain world in a constant state of flux. This is especially true of the foreign exchange market. Exchange rates can and do move rapidly and unpredictably by large amounts in relatively short periods of time. As with share options, currency options may be used as hedging instruments. The call option will hedge against the risk of an appreciation of the foreign currency that the option holder may wish to purchase some time during the life of the option. The put option hedges the opposite risk, the possibility of a fall in the value of the currency that I may wish to sell some time in the future. One may use such options to 'lock in' to known fixed rates today. Such options are likely to be attractive to, for example, companies in the export or import trade who earn their cash flow in one currency and keep their accounts in another.

As a British exporter to the United States, I earn my cash flow from exports most likely in dollars but assess the profitability of my business in sterling. If the market is keenly competitive, my profit margin on my export contracts may be under pressure, leaving little margin to absorb a drop in the sterling proceeds of the sales in the event of an appreciation of sterling against the dollar between

Table 6.6 Currency option: Philadelphia Exchange; pound against the dollar

Underlying price, i.e. the current exchange rate as at 5.4.1984: £1 = 144.65c, i.e. £1 = 1.4465

Strike price, i.e. the price at which the holder of the call option may purchase the currency or the put option holder sell the currency	Option premiums					
	Calls, i.e buys £s			Puts, i.e. sells £s		
	June	September	December	June	September	December
145c	–	4.10c	6.30c	2.60c	–	–
150c	1.00c	–	–	–	–	–
155c	–	1.00c	–	–	–	–

– no contracts traded at this price. All contracts are integral multiples of £12,500.

concluding a dollar-priced contract and actually receiving the dollars.

A currency option contract is a way of buying insurance against such an adverse movement in the exchange rate. The June 150 Call premium of 1c per pound would enable such an exporter to fix the effective exchange rate now at $1.50 = £1.

An American exporter pricing in sterling for the UK market can fix his dollar receipts in exchange for the sterling proceeds of the contract by buying a sterling put. For a premium of 2.60c payable now, he can fix a price of $1.45 = £1. If exercised, the effective exchange rate would be the strike price less the premium, that is, $1.45 - 2.60c = $1.424.

As the standard contract size is for £12,500, a total of 80 such currency option contracts would be required to cover a £1m contract. The cost of this for a June 150 Call would then be 80 × 12,500 × 1c = $10,000.

Thus, exporters and importers concerned with the exchange rate between sterling and the dollar can fix an exchange rate between the two currencies possibly even in advance of signing a contract for the supply of goods and services. They can effectively hedge or protect themselves against adverse exchange rate movements.

A major advantage of this type of contract is its option nature–it may be, but does not have to be, exercised. If I earn dollars and want pounds sterling, I may have a June 150 call option. If, when I receive the dollars, the market rate available to me is $1.40 = £1, I would choose to sell my dollars on the foreign-exchange spot market rather than exercise the currency option. The option would have no intrinsic value: it would be out of the money but might just have some time value and could itself be traded for its residual time value premium.

It is a flexible instrument compared to other means of protecting oneself against foreign-exchange risks. The option nature that leaves the decision to the holder whether it should be exercised, traded or allowed to expire, allows much more leeway in decision making than other methods of insuring against such risks.

Forward exchange contracts arranged through banks impose an obligation to buy or sell the currency at the agreed rate on the predetermined date. The only option element normally possible in these contracts is the option as to precisely when in a predetermined future period of time, delivery of the currency to the bank will be made or taken. The contracts are not optional as to whether obligations are performed, only as to precisely when within stated time limits.

Currency option contracts have many other advantages shared generally with other option contracts. For buyers–holders of such option contracts–the maximum loss if the contract is not exercised and is allowed to expire without being traded is the premium. This aspect makes these contracts in some respects very much like an insurance policy. In both cases, the premium paid can be thought of as producing a return in the form of protection against an adverse event happening that would lead to the cover being demanded. The fire insurance premium on the factory thus has similarities with the option premium that protects the sterling receipts of the company's dollar export trade.

The negotiable nature of the instrument provides an added dimension of flexibility enabling it to be sold. This in itself can be a source of profit as premiums can change rapidly by large percentage amounts.

There are disadvantages to these option currency contracts. Inspection of Table 6.6 shows a market in a relatively early stage of development. Only three possible exchange rates are covered and options are only available on five of the eighteen possible combinations of rate and maturity dates. This is a fluctuating situation. It is just possible that it would be impossible to 'trade' the traded option depending on how prices moved between its acquisition and the decision to sell. This potential disadvantage may disappear if the instrument becomes more popular and the market develops.

The option is of course no investment *per se*. It does not produce a direct return. If not exercised or traded before expiry, it becomes worthless. It is simply a premium paid in return for the option to acquire an asset at an agreed strike price during the life of the option. If the prices of the underlying securities, shares and exchange rates in the two examples discussed in detail above, move so that the option is simply not worth exercising, the premium will be lost. Gain is thus conditional, for the holder of the option, generally on call option underlying prices rising and put option underlying prices falling.

Speculators may be more interested in the rapidly fluctuating premiums that characterise these option markets rather than in the hedging facilities that are provided for those whose business requires them to take a keen interest in exchange rate movements. Speculative interest may also be centred on, for example, the possibility of acquiring currency or shares via an option exercise at prices below current market rates allowing for a profit on subsequent sale on the spot market.

Leverage

All of us have but limited finance. If one has £1,000 to invest and the underlying price of a share we fancy is £5, one could only purchase 200 shares with the funds at one's disposal.

One may anticipate a sharp rise in the price of this share and therefore choose to buy say a £4.50 call option at a premium of £1 per share.

By using the Traded Options Market in this way, one could either acquire options on 1,000 shares with the funds at one's disposal or spend say £200 on options, leaving £800 to finance other ventures. If the price of the underlying shares rises to say £6 before the expiry of the option, one might typically be able to sell the option at a premium of £2.50 per share. Deducting the £1 premium originally paid, this leaves a profit of £1.50 or return of 150%.

Alternatively, the option could be exercised, the effective price of so doing being the sum of the premium and the option exercise price. This amounts to £5.50. Selling the shares thus acquired at a price of £6 leaves a total profit, ignoring transaction costs, of 1000 × £0.50 = £500 or 50%.

These percentages are possible over relatively short periods of time and would be very much greater if calculated on an annualised basis. The illustrative calculations above also show that trading the option is often a way to produce higher returns than exercising the option itself.

Leverage is a means of accomplishing power or influence. It is used as a term in the Traded Options Market to refer to buying and selling options to achieve command over a larger number of shares than one's own resources would permit if options were not available.

Notes

1 J. Parnell, 'How the ordinary investor can use options', *Investors*

Chronicle, 6 January 1984, p. 18.

2　The advantages of this will depend upon the particular tax position of the option buyer.

3　Transaction costs on traded options are normally quite small, often around 1/10 of 1% of the value of the underlying contract. If only a small number of shares have to be bought by a naked option writer, these costs may be considerable and further significantly increase the costs of having the option exercised against him.

4　In the language of the foreign-exchange market, spot rates are for delivery normally 2 trading days hence. They are thus different from rates for 'same day' delivery.

Chapter Seven

Investment trusts and unit trusts

Buying shares in only a few companies carries an associated risk of loss arising from declining markets for their products and any managerial inadequacies. This type of risk can be avoided by constructing a portfolio of shares from a wide range of companies operating in different product and trading areas. The obvious difficulty here is that many, if not most, individual investors are unlikely to possess sufficient funds to acquire such a range of direct investments.

The presence of any problems in financial markets tends to generate solutions. The problems of achieving a broad-based portfolio with limited financial resources gives rise to the *investment trust* and the *unit trust*.

These two quite distinct types of trust are often confused but are quite different except in so far as both are means of buying the protection offered by a diversified portfolio that would not be possible for an individual to acquire by direct share buying. Both forms of trust enable individuals to benefit from the managerial expertise responsible for the trust's buying and selling decisions.

Investment trusts

The form of the printout of data relating to investment trusts in the financial press immediately suggests the nature of such trusts. Consider the data relating to one such trust, the Ailsa Investment Trust PLC, in Table 7.1.

Table 7.1 Printout data for an investment trust, 1985

High	Low	Price	+/−	Net dividend	Cover	Gross yield
101	87	91	−1	1.8p	1.4	2.8

Source: *Financial Times*, 25 September 1985

This printout of summary statistical information is of an identical form to that of the Midland Bank and Cadbury Schweppes considered in Chapter 5, The Evaluation of a Company. Investment trusts are thus companies with much in common with Stock Exchange listed companies in manufacturing, services, retailing and distribution. On buying into an investment trust, one becomes a shareholder in precisely the same way as when shares in any other company are acquired. The data summarised here is thus to be read in exactly the same way as for any other type of company.

The last dividend paid was 1.8p per share. The tax credit equal to the current 30% standard rate of tax may be shown to be 0.77p per share.[1]

The gross yield of 2.8% is also calculated as shown in greater detail in Chapter 5.[2] It should be noted that the price of 91p per share used in these calculations is a mid-market price, that is, the price midway between the buying and selling prices of the share in question. Thus, the yield shown in this summary is higher than the yield attainable by anyone buying at the price used in the calculation of the 91p per share shown.

The dividend cover ratio of 1.4 is the ratio of earnings per share to dividend paid. A ratio of 1.4 indicates that its reciprocal, 1/1.4 or 71% of earnings has been paid out as dividend and 29% retained within the trust.[3]

The use of these statistics as an aid to understanding the company's financial position has already been considered in detail. It is repeated here for an investment trust to emphasise just how like other companies investment trusts really are.

We turn now to consider published data that reflects more the special characteristics of investment trusts. The earnings of investment trusts are derived, not from manufacturing activity, the provision of services, or the distribution of goods and services produced by others, but broadly by the investing of money either by investing money in the shares of other companies or by fixed interest loans through the acquisition of government securities.[4]

The earnings of investment trusts are thus derived from the trading activities and profits of those companies whose shares constitute the trusts' portfolios. The various trusts pursue quite radically different policies both as to the geographical areas of the world in which they will invest and the sectors of activity that are represented in their portfolios.

The Ailsa Investment Trust PLC listed above, for example, invests 42.4% of its portfolio in the UK, 32% in North America, and 26.4% in consumer groups compared to 21.1% in capital goods.[4] In thinking about an investment in this particular trust, we would have to consider whether these spreads corresponded to where we think growth lies in the future. Geographical and sector spreads vary so radically between the different trusts that one may well expect to find one or even several trusts whose spreads coincide with just about any view as to what is expected to grow most rapidly in the future. Do we fancy the UK, North America, Japan, or other areas? Trusts exist that specialise predominantly in one or other of these areas, or in a spread of two or more.

Scanning the summary financial data on investment trusts shows certain trusts for which only a current share price is shown. As should be clear from the calculations above, this must mean no dividend has been paid and hence such statistics as the net dividend, cover ratio and gross yield have no meaning and cannot be calculated.

This does not mean that such a trust would necessarily be a poorer investment than those actually paying dividends. It may arise from the very nature of the trust itself. An example is the Cystic Fibrosis Research Investment Trust PLC.

This was set up in 1981 to provide financial assistance for research into cystic fibrosis, a respiratory disease that affects children. £280,000 of 5% debentures were issued together with an issue of some 520,000 £1 shares. The debenture interest is paid as normal but no dividends are paid to the shareholders. The attraction of such a trust, apart from sympathy for its charitable aims, lies in increases in the asset value of the trust being reflected in the share price. Such an arrangement would be of particular interest to higher-rate income tax payers interested in capital gains.[5]

Over the 4-year period 1981–5 the share price rose from a 1981 low of 85p to a 1985 high of 320p, a capital appreciation of 276%.[6] This is the major attraction for a non-dividend paying trust. Thus, reading the published financial information in newspapers may need supplementing from other sources if a fuller understanding of the summary statistics is to be obtained.

Net asset value of an investment trust

If an individual owns property and other assets worth £30,000 and has debts of £10,000, then his net asset value is clearly £20,000. This example is analogous to the net asset value of an investment trust.

The gross asset value of an investment trust is analogous to the totality of an individual's assets. It is represented by its shareholdings in other companies and is thus the investment that generates the income of the trust. From this total is then deducted any liabilities such as borrowings, and thus the net asset value is derived. Dividing this figure by the total number of shares produces the published statistic, net asset value per share.

The net asset value per share is thus the profit-earning figure per share that generates the income and provides for future capital growth. Growth over time in the net asset value per share is one measurement of how effectively the trust is being managed. As the general state of the relevant economies affects the growth of the net

Table 7.2 Investment trusts: share prices and net asset values

Year	Trust	Share price	Net asset value per share	Comment
1984	Ailsa Inv. Trust PLC	68p	92.9p	discount of 24.9p = 26.80% on n.a.v.
1984	GT Japan IT PLC	144p	144p	zero. neither premium nor discount
1984	Shires Inv. PLC	217p	192.3p	share price premium of 24.7p = 12.84% on n.a.v.

Source: AITC *How to Make IT*, Guide to Investment Trusts 1985/6

asset value, it is better regarded as a judgement of management when compared to other trusts with broadly similar objectives. Whilst the concept of net asset value per share may be applied to any type of company, it is with reference to investment trusts that the figure is published.

Buying a share in an investment trust is buying the ownership, but not the control of an amount of profit-earning assets equal to the net asset value per share. This leads naturally to a comparison of the share price to the net asset value. They are not normally the same. If the share price is less than the net asset value per share, then the former stands at a discount in relationship to the latter and, if the share price is greater than the net asset value, then the former stands at a premium to the net asset value. Illustrative examples are shown in Table 7.2.

It is interesting to ask the question, how these differences arise. A simplistic view would suggest purchasing investment trust shares so as to acquire net asset value as cheaply as possible, that is, in those trusts with the biggest discounts. The assumption behind this strategy would be that net asset value is homogeneous, that is, net asset value units in one investment trust are the same as such units in any other trust. This is clearly not so. The investor may be prepared to pay more for units of net asset value in trusts he fancies for their future growth prospects than for the net asset value of trusts specialising in companies and areas of the world that he views as relatively less attractive. Differing views of this nature result in the coexistence over time of different share price to net asset value ratios, that is, to discounts and premiums. This is similar in some respects to the existence over time of radically different price/earnings ratios.

Looking through tables of investment trust data, it is discounts that predominate: £1 of net asset value typically costs less than £1 to acquire. This is claimed as a major advantage of such trusts over other forms of investment. It means that each £1 spent on acquiring such shares results in the ownership being acquired of more than £1 of net asset value and the investment actually at work earning dividends and hopefully producing capital growth for the future then exceeds the cost of purchase.

Gearing factors
These statistics are published in a number of sources but commonly

at monthly intervals in the financial press on the basis of data supplied by the Association of Investment Trust Companies.

The formal definition of the *gearing factor* is that it indicates in percentage terms the amount by which the net asset value of a trust would rise if the value of its equity assets rose by 100%, that is, doubled in value. It is thus a particular measurement of the sensitivity of the net asset value to a change in equity prices. Such a statistic is useful if we are considering the acquisition of investment trust shares and have a view about the likely movements of the prices of equities in the near future. A high gearing factor would be attractive if we anticipate general bull market conditions in equity markets, and possibly an indicator of a trust to avoid if we are convinced that a sharp decline in equity prices is 'just around the corner'.

The gross asset value of an investment trust is its earnings base. This may be in a range of different types of income-earning assets. Typically, one finds varying percentages of equities, UK and foreign government fixed interest stocks, foreign currency denominated bonds, and even shares in other investment trusts. The proportions will vary depending upon the aims of the particular trust and the related investment decisions made by the trust managers.

Trusts will also have varying liabilities in the form of debts. They may have issued varying amounts of debentures or have currency borrowings. As already defined above, the net asset value of the trust is the gross value minus liabilities for debt payments. Now what will happen to the net asset value if the equity components uniformly double in value? The answer would be the same as for the gross asset value if liabilities were zero. Consider an investment trust with 50% of its investments by value in equities and 50% in fixed interest government stocks. A doubling of equity prices would increase the gross asset value to 150% of its pre-price-increase value, an increase of 50%. A few simple similar calculations will show that, with these restrictive assumptions, the gross asset value will rise by an amount equal to the proportion by value of equities in the trust's portfolio before the price increases take place.

In the three examples considered below, the data remains constant except for variations in the percentage of the gross asset value that is assumed to consist of equity holdings. This enables us to follow the variations in the net asset value per share as, other things remaining constant, the assumed equity percentage composition of the gross asset value alters.

Worked examples

The basic equation is:

$$\text{Net asset value per share} = \frac{\text{Gross assets} - \text{liabilities}}{\text{Number of shares}}$$

By way of an initial value, assume that gross assets equal £10m, liabilities £2m, and that there are 16 million shares in the trust. Substituting these figures into the above formula shows the net asset value per share to be 50p. From a consideration of the terms of the formula and how they relate one to the other, it should be clear that the effect on net asset value per share of a rise in equity prices will depend upon the proportion of gross assets held in the form of such equities.

(i)   Assume that we know that the £10m assets above consist of £8m equities and the balance in fixed interest bearing securities. What will be the effect on the net asset value per share if equity values now double? The reader should verify that the new value is

$$\frac{£ (8\text{m} \times 2) + £2\text{m} - £2\text{m}}{16\text{m}}$$

= £1   net asset value per share (a rise of 100% from the initial 50p per share derived from a doubling in value of less than 100% of the value of the gross assets)

(ii) In this second example, vary the asset composition again so that the £10m is made up of £1m equities and £9m fixed interest bearing securities. As before, equity prices now double. The new net asset value per share is:

$$= \frac{(£ (1\text{m} \times 2) + 9 - £2\text{m})}{16\text{m}}$$

= 56.25p net asset value per share, that is, a rise of 12.5% in the figure following a doubling in the value of 10% of the initial value of gross assets

(iii) In this final example, assume that the entire £10m is held in the form of equities and nothing in the form of fixed interest bearing securities. A doubling in equity values now changes the net asset value per share to:

$$= \frac{(£(10m \times 2) - £2m)}{16m}$$

= £1.125 new net asset value per share, that is, a 125% rise in the figure following a 100% increase in the prices of the 100% of gross assets.

As the above formula shows, the net asset value per share will vary, not only as equity prices change, but also as the liabilities of the trust and the number of shares issued also vary. Summarising the results obtained above into Table 7.3 illustrates the use of the word 'gearing' or its American equivalent 'leverage'.

Table 7.3 Illustration of gearing

% of gross assets held in the form of equities	Effect on the net asset value per share of a doubling of equity prices, i.e. the gearing factor (%)
10	12.5
80	100.0
100	125.0

In each case, the effect on the net asset value per share shown in the second column is greater than the percentage of gross assets held in the form of equities. The use of the term 'gearing' occurs in several places in the discussion of financial statistics. In all cases, its general meaning is that one change has an effect on something else, the effect being some multiple of the cause. In this specific example, the percentage of assets held in the form of equities determines the effect on net asset value of a doubling of equity prices.

Warrants

A glance at the statistical summaries on investment trusts in the financial press shows both a quoted price for the shares of each trust and, for certain trusts, an additional quotation for warrants. Consider the example below:

	Price
Consolidated Venture Trust	93p
100 warrants	23p
120 warrants	21p

Source: *Financial Times*, 25 September 1985

The warrant has properties akin to call options on the Traded Options Market. The warrant itself is marketable and is a right, but not an obligation, to acquire shares in the trust at a stated price during a predetermined period of time.

The Consolidated Venture Trust warrants in the above example are rights to buy ordinary shares in the trust at prices respectively of 100p and 120p exercisable each year during the month following the despatch of accounts for the financial years ending 31 January 1986–90 in the case of the 100p warrants and to 31 January 1986–93 in the case of the 120p warrants.[7]

How attractive are such warrants? The total cost of buying shares this way is the warrant cost plus the exercise price, a total of 123p for the 100p warrants and 141p for the 120p warrants. This compares to a current share price of 93p.

Warrants are thus not the cheapest way of currently acquiring these shares. However, one is buying time and fixing now the total cost of buying shares until 1993 in the case of the 120p warrants. What if by 1993 the share price is 200p? Approximately four warrants can currently be acquired for the price of one share–a gearing of 4:1. If share prices rise sufficiently, limited funds would allow the investor to exercise his warrants, acquire and resell four times the number that would be possible if he were to buy the shares at the current price. The 'general consensus' or the 'average view' embodied in the prices is that the share price will be significantly higher between now and 1993 than it is at present.

The warrants become shares only when exercised. On being exercised, the warrants become shares on a 1:1 basis. As such, the net asset value per share will be reduced. Two million of these particular warrants were issued, each time involving if exercised in total an increase of 10% in the ordinary capital of the trust and thus, other things being equal, to a 10% reduction in net asset value per share. Profitable deployment of the extra funds received on exercise of the conversion right would tend to increase the net asset value per share.

Unit trusts

Unit trusts and investment trusts have one major feature in common. Both offer investments that reduce risks by choosing a spread of investments but, otherwise, there are considerable differences.

The purchaser of investment trust shares becomes a part-owner of the trust. He owns the assets of the trust in proportion to his shareholdings and, although in practice, he may not control the investment decisions of the trust, he has all the powers of shareholders in companies in other areas. The unit trust investor owns his units but he is not a shareholder and hence not an owner of the trust whose units he buys.

Investment trust share prices are fixed by the forces of supply and demand on the Stock Exchange and the influence of one individual on the price would normally be minimal. In the case of the unit trust, it is the manager of the trust who fixes the buying and selling prices of the units, or the *bid* and *offer* prices as they are technically known. The printed summary statistical information on unit and investment trusts reflects this distinction. The single quoted price for investment trust shares follows the practice applied to share prices generally: the middle-market price is printed, that is, the price midway between the buying price and selling price. Unit trust data normally includes both the current bid price, the price at which the trust will buy back its units from investors, and the offer price, the price at which the trust's manager will sell the units to the public. It would of course be perfectly possible for both forms of trust to present their price information in a common format. A middle price for unit trusts' units could be obtained by simply averaging the bid and offer prices, or both the prices averaged to obtain the middle-market price could be printed in the case of investment trusts. However, that is not the way things are done and the unit trust data is reported as in the example below (Table 7.4).

Note first the name of the company offering the units. There may be an investment choice to be made between the shares of the company offering the units and the units themselves. As a specific example of a fairly general situation, one could choose say between the shares of the finance company Aitken Hume with the rights attaching to owners of ordinary shares in listed companies, and buying the 'product' of the company, namely the units of the various types on offer. In the latter case, of course, one would have none of the rights of ordinary shareholders.

Table 7.4 Example of unit trust summary financial reporting: Aitken Hume

Unit trust fund	Bid price	Offer price	Gross yield
American Technical	96p	102.7	–
Fund Jap Technology	50.4p	58.9	0.10

Source: adapted from *Unit Trust Yearbook*, 1985

There are a number of points to notice. In considering the likely financial gain over a period of years, one would concentrate on the likely change from the cost of acquisition now (the offer price), to the future likely price at which the investor could sell his units (the bid price).

It is also interesting to compare the gross yields offered to the yields on equities generally. Generally, the yields both on investment trust shares and on unit trust holdings are less than on equities generally. The general expectation is obviously that the discrepancy reflects the expectations of faster and more secure growth of such investments than is likely for direct equity investments.

Unit prices
The price of units is closely controlled by the required use of a formula approved by the Department of Trade and Industry. Clearly, bid and offer prices, the prices at which the unit trust

managers will buy back from and sell to holders of the units will reflect the market values of the underlying securities, that is, the prices will reflect the investments made with the funds. The formula is applied by calculating a maximum price at which the units may be offered for sale, the offer price, and a minimum price at which the managers may buy back the units from their holders, the bid price. There is no restriction on lower offer prices and/or higher bid prices. These boundary maximum and minimum prices act to protect investors in unit trusts from any unit pricing that is unrelated to the value of the underlying assets of the trust.

Calculation of a boundary: maximum offer price

Value of the securities in the fund at the lowest market dealing offer for sale prices in the recognised stock markets is £5m. On the 10 million units in the fund, this represents a value of securities per unit of	50.000p
Add 1% stamp duty (0.500p), brokerage and contract stamp (0.625p), and unit trust instrument duty at ¼% (0.125p)	1.250p
Add accrued income (0.2000p per unit) and 5% initial charge (2.572p)	2.772p
Add rounding off (1% maximum = 0.545p)	0.540
Offer price per unit according to Department of Trade formula	54.562p
Published offer price with inescapable minimum additional rounding):	54.500p

Source: adapted from *Unit Trust Yearbook*, 1985

These prices can be graphed as in Figure 7.1 to make the significance of them clearer.

Bid and offer prices for units are quoted regularly in the financial press but how does one know whether the prices quoted are fair market prices in the sense that they bear a close relationship to the value of the underlying securities?

The answer is that the managements of unit trusts have to use a

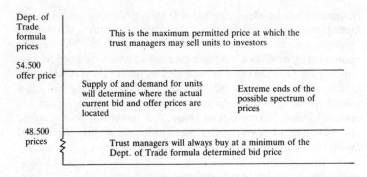

Figure 7.1   Calculation of a boundary

Department of Trade approved formula to establish a minimum bid price , a minimum price at which they will buy back units from investors, and also a maximum offer price, a maximum price at which they will sell units to investors. They may, of course, quote higher bid prices and lower offer prices but the Department of Trade formula ensures that boundaries are established to the possible spectrum of prices and that the boundaries will relate to the market values of the individual securities in which the trusts have invested their pooled funds.

Calculation of a boundary: minimum bid price

Value of securities in the fund at the highest market dealing bid or buying prices offered to investors wishing to sell is £4.9m. On 10 million units in the fund, this represents a value of securites per unit of   49.000p

Add accrued income, for example, from equities and gilts in which the fund is invested: £20,000. On 10 million units, this amounts to 0.200 p per unit: 0.200p

Subtract brokerage and contract stamp 0.615p per unit and also a rounding-off amount of 0.085p per unit (Rounding off maximum of 1% would be 0.486p per unit)   0.700p

Bid price per unit according to Department of Trade
formula   48.500p

Source: adapted from *Unit Trust Yearbook 1985*

It may not be unreasonable to expect a fairly close association or
correlation in the movement of 'general unit' prices and movements
in a related Stock Market index. Both are made up by a process of
averaging individual share price changes over a given period of
time. Although the units may well not and, indeed, are most likely
not to exactly reflect the share composition of a particular index, the
averaging process itself seems to result in practice in a fairly close
association in the movements of the respective averages. These
relationships are often quite robust to differences in their respective
compositions. This is shown in Figure 7.2 for the specific example of
the TSB General Unit Trust.[8]

Unit trust managers sometimes advertise their management skills
by reference to the growth in the value of the units over a period of

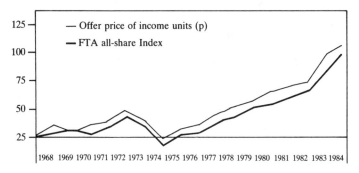

Figure 7.2 TSB General Unit Trust: offer price of units (p) and the FTA
All-share Index 1968–1987

Source: *C. Michelmore Explores the world of Unit Trusts with TSB*, TSB
1985

time in the past. It should be clear that if the graph of any particular units in relationship to an associated share price index moves as in the diagram, then no particular skill is necessarily required to achieve such a result. Simply investing in the spread of shares as weighted in the relevant index would achieve a similar result.

Such a graph should also act as a warning to anyone who buys units as a protection against long-term erosion of capital due to inflation. Annual inflation rates over the last forty years have always been positive, that is, the general price level has risen continuously upwards and hence the value of money in terms of its purchasing power has moved inexorably downwards. Share prices and thus unit values have fluctuated over the same period, rising with successive 'bull' markets and falling with the following 'bear' phases of the markets. Because of this, unit values correlate poorly over time with cost of living indices and offer no guarantee of protection against inflation. For those who require certain protection against inflation, equities and unit trusts should generally be avoided and securities with index-linked capital and/or income considered. Exactly the same reasoning would cause investments trusts to be avoided by those unable or unwilling to jeopardise capital.

What has been written about closely correlated unit values and share price indices applies to general equity trusts. At the time of writing, early 1987, 'special situation' funds are becoming increasing offered and to these, these observations do not apply. With such funds, the managers may back hunches and invest in a spread of shares radically different from the spread represented in the index. The managers may be looking for shares likely to rise sharply in value due to a takeover, changes in management or moving into new, profitable markets. In all these situations, the possibility of high capital gains is offset by a possibility of capital loss. These 'special situations' trusts deliberately in the pursuit of high gains forgo the protection against large losses that a broad spread of shares provides; they are thus much riskier investments.

Net asset value and share price

Some investment trusts have a fixed winding-up date for the trust built into the initial flotation terms. Others may make provision for an annual vote on 'winding up' of the trust. On winding up, net asset value (NAV) would be realised and distributed to its owners, the shareholders.

One consequence of such a provision is a likely reduction in the discount or premium attached to the price in relationship to the NAV per share. A winding-up arrangement may explicitly be included in the 'offer for sale' for this very reason.[9]

Another recent development

For some time, investment trusts have included 'trusts of trusts'– trusts that have invested wholly or in part in other trusts. Unit trusts are now allowed to establish these master funds or funds of funds.

They are at first glance attractive. Investing in a number of subsidiary funds taps the managerial expertise of the subsidiaries. Unfortunately, managerial expertise is not always of one mind! Shifting between funds costs money as well as running the risk of alienating their subsidiary fund managers by these antics. These factors may well more than offset the assumed benefits of a wider pool of available managerial expertise.

Notes

1 Let x equal the gross dividend corresponding to the recorded net dividend of 1.8p per share. As the standard rate of income tax is deducted from the gross dividend before payment is made and is at the present standard rate of 30% or 0.3, then $0.7x = 1.8$p, $x = 1.8-/0.7 = 2.57-$ gross dividend.

   The tax credit is equal to the gross dividend minus the net dividend or $2.57p - 1.8p = 0.77p$ per share.

2 The gross yield is equal to (gross dividend in pence per share/quoted middle price) 100.

   Substituting into the equation the known data, the gross yield now is $(2.57p/91)100 = 2.8\%$ shown in the final column of Table 7.1.

3 Cover ratio calculations are more involved than this brief summary suggests. The reader is referred to the extended discussion on this topic in Chapter 5.

4 A useful source of information on the investments of these trusts is the Trade Association of the Investment Trusts, The Association of Investment Trust Companies. For example, the 1985/6 edition of *How To Make IT*, published by the association, gives considerable detail on the types of securities held by those trusts that are members of the

association. The distribution between the various categories of investments differs according to the aims of each trust.

5 For details of comments on this and other securities, see the 'cards' published by McCarthy Information Ltd.

6 See 'Extel Card' on the trust published by the Extel UK Listed Companies Service.

7 *How To Make IT*, 1985/6 edition, p. 72. See note 6.

8 Financial Times Actuaries All-share Index is another index used to average share prices in addition to those considered in previous chapters.Its behaviour over time normally follows closely that of the FT 30 Share Index.

9 'In an endeavour to maintain the value of the Ordinary Shares as against the net asset value of the Company, the Articles of Association of the Company contain provisions for the winding-up of the Company', The German Securities Investments Trust PLC Offer for Subscription, November 1985.

Chapter Eight

The markets for foreign currencies

Exchange rates

An exchange rate between any two currencies may be thought of as the price of one currency in terms of the other. In the world of the 1980s, despite the attempts at stabilisation represented for example by the International Monetary Fund and the European Monetary System, these rates move, sometimes oscillating around a particular value, at other times moving rapidly up or down.

Quite dramatic changes in relative values do still occur over fairly short periods of time. One of the most dramatic current examples is probably the variation in the $/£ exchange rate over the period from 1974 to the time of writing in January 1987, Figure 8.1.

The first part of this chapter looks at how exchange rates are determined and then at the consequences of the uncertainties of this market for exporters and importers, and the nature of the hedging possibilities available to meet the risks inherent in incurring costs of production in one currency and revenue from sales in another.

How exchange rates are determined

The exchange rate between sterling and the United States dollar is determined by the demand for pounds by holders of dollars compared to the demand for dollars by holders of pounds. The demand for pounds has, therefore, an implied supply of dollars and the demand for dollars an implied supply of pounds. Thus, we may construct two diagrams, one showing the value of the dollar in terms of pounds and the other, the reciprocal of the first, the value of the pound in terms of dollars. The diagrams are shown in Figure 8.2.

The diagrams are inextricably linked, the one cannot exist

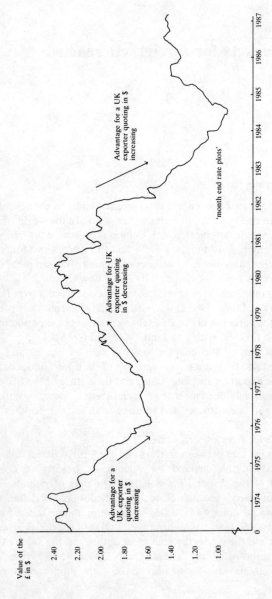

Value of the
£ in $

2.40
2.20
2.00
1.80
1.60
1.40
1.20
1.00

0

Advantage for a
UK exporter
quoting in $
increasing

Advantage for UK
exporter quoting
in $ decreasing

Advantage for a UK
exporter quoting in $
increasing

'month end rate plots'

1974 1975 1976 1977 1978 1979 1980 1981 1982 1983 1984 1985 1986 1987

Figure 8.1 Variations in the dollar/pound exchange rate 1974–1987

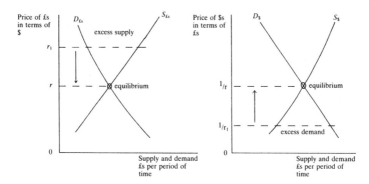

Figure 8.2 Determination of exchange rates

without the other. The 'excess demand' for dollars in the right-hand diagram driving up the price of dollars from $1/r$ to $1/r_1$ is simply another way of showing the information in the left-hand diagram with its counterpart 'excess supply' of pounds driving the price of pounds down from r to r_1. The system is equilibrium-seeking in that the forces present in the market drive rates towards the intersection points of the supply and demand curves. Before equilibrium is attained, it is likely that disturbance factors will have determined another equilibrium point. That is why the term 'equilibrium-seeking' is to be preferred to 'equilibrium-attaining'.

The graph Figure 8.1, showing the behaviour of the sterling/dollar exchange rate over a 10-year period may be viewed as tracing out the equilibrium point of the left-hand diagram. The very act of drawing graphs and diagrams in two dimensions implies a static market with the forces in the market summarised in the static position of the lines drawn. Nothing could be further from the truth. The nature of the forces is such that the curves and lines are best viewed as continuously moving.

The 'human factor' in rate adjustment

The diagrams referred to above imply an impersonal market. In one sense, it is. Single buyers and sellers are seldom if ever large enough to affect market rates by the volume or value of their own transactions. However, rate adjustments are made by foreign exchange dealers in response to changes in the demand and supply

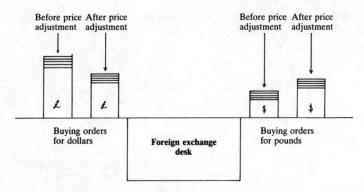

Figure 8.3 The foreign exchange dealer at his desk

of the traded currencies. The electronic communications between market centres linking dealers ensure that the simplification of one equilibrium rate as shown in the diagrams is not too far removed from reality at any particular point of time.

A crude but instructive oversimplification may help to indicate how supply and demand forces actually work. Imagine a pre-electronic foreign exchange dealer at his desk. The situations shown in the diagrams translate into buying orders for dollars piling up on the desk: See Figure 8.3

The increased demand for the dollar is reflected in the pounds piling up on his desk. What is he to do? He is running low on dollars. If he increases the price of dollars and decreases the price of pounds, more dollars will flow on to the market and fewer dollars will be demanded. Thus, human agents adjust prices in response to currency flow imbalance and so exchange rates are altered.

Arbitrage

One of the simplifications in the above example is that our attention has been restricted to a two-currency model. There are obviously dozens of currencies actively traded. They are linked via a process known as *arbitrage*.

Consider the three-currency example of Figure 8.4. It may appear obvious that, if $2 = £1 and £1 = 4 DM, then $1 must also equal 2 DM. This would not necessarily be the case in the absence of the

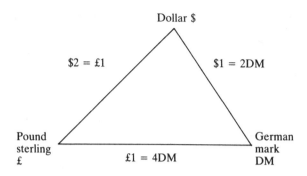

Figure 8.4   Arbitrage in a three-currency system

arbitrageur. The demand and supply curves for the various currencies may very well establish bilateral rates that are not simultaneously equilibrium rates all the way round a triangle such as in the figure. If the dollar/mark rate were initially $1 = 1.90 DM, then a profitable opportunity would exist to shift funds to take advantage of the rate being 'out of line' with other rates. It is this moving of funds to take advantage of rate anomalies that is known as arbitrage.

Profitable arbitrage exists in this situation with an initial dollar/mark rate of $1 = 1.90 DM. This is shown below. Use dollars to buy pounds and then use pounds to buy marks. One dollar will buy 1.90 DM but it will also buy £0.50, which, in its turn, will buy 2.00 DM. As long as rates are out of line by more than the transaction costs of moving funds, profitable arbitrage will exist and will pull the rates back into line to the point where costs prevent minor discrepancies being profitably exploited.

Significance of the Foreign Exchange Market to exporting companies

Consider a company exporting in a highly competitive market. If it is UK-based and exporting to the United States, its costs of production will be in sterling and its revenue in dollars assuming that the American customers require price quotations in their domestic currency. Typically, cost will be incurred in advance of payment being received.

In this situation, the profitability of the contract depends entirely upon the sterling/dollar exchange rate. Consider the following example.

A contract has been signed to supply goods to the United States. The costs of production were £500,000 and the selling price was $1,000,000. The exchange rate assumed was $1.67 = £1. If this rate holds until payment is made, the sterling equivalent of the million dollars will be £600,000 and thus a profit of 20% will be made on the contract.

If, before payment is received, the rate falls to $1.20 = £1, an appreciation of the dollar and depreciation of the pound, then the sterling proceeds of the dollar price will rise to £833,333 to yield a profit of 67%. An appreciation of sterling to say $2 = £1 would reduce the sterling proceeds to £500,000 to completely wipe out the profit on the contract. A rise of $2.4 = £1 would mean sterling proceeds of £416,667 and a loss of 16.7%. The rates used in this example are all rates that have existed on the market at some time between 1974 and 1987. Figure 8.1 shows the periods of time when sterling has been generally falling against the dollar. These are the periods in which extra profits would have accrued to UK exporters quoting in dollars. There have also been periods when quoting in dollars would have severely reduced the profits of exporters to the United States.

Thus, such contracts have an exchange risk. In the example used here, an appreciation of the domestic currency of the exporter against the currency of the importer reduces the profits and any fall would of course enhance the profit margin.

Consider an exchange rate of $2.28 = £1 and the expectation that the pound will strengthen further. What should be done with $1,000,000,000 of the company's dollar reserves? Sell the dollars and buy pounds to produce a sterling reserve of £439m. However, shortly afterwards, sterling falls to $1.46 = £1. Moving from dollars into pounds at this rate would produce £685m, a 'loss' of some £246m. This particular mistake by the Rolls-Royce company contributed to the financial collapse of the company reported in 1983.[1]

The consequences of exchange rate movements for the earnings per share of a company are fairly obvious. Companies based in the United States and exporting to countries whose currencies are depreciating against the dollar will lose earnings that will depend on the proportion of the company's sales made abroad. Thus, a company such as Coca Cola with around 60% of its sales abroad will be particularly affected.

For companies located in countries whose currencies are depreciating against the dollar, exchange rate movements enhance earnings, again in proportion both to the rate movement and to the percentage of its output sold to the appreciating currency area.

Such a prolonged appreciation of the dollar has led to a critical hindsight reappraisal of the wisdom of borrowing dollars.

A principle to guide the choice of the particular currency to be borrowed that is often stressed as sound financial sense is that we should always borrow the currency in which the cash flow will be earned. Thus, if our investment will earn dollars, then we borrow dollars to finance its construction and development. In this way, we eliminate the exchange risk that attaches to financing in one currency an investment that will earn its revenue denominated in another.

Clearly, given the variation in the sterling/dollar exchange rate shown over the 10 years from 1974 to 1984 in Figure 8.1, it would have been advantageous for a dollar earner to have financed his capital projects aimed at the American market out of sterling borrowings. Inspection of the figure will show that appropriate timing of borrowings and repayment could have halved the dollar value of sterling borrowings. This would have involved borrowing sterling to finance a dollar-earning project when the rate of exchange was $2.4 = £1 and repaying the borrowings at a rate of $1.2 = £1. Only one-half of the originally estimated dollar amount would have been required to buy the sterling to repay the sterling loan. This would have been akin to finding that you had suddenly been offered a 50% discount on the outstanding loan amount. Quite a bonus!

It will be equally clear that it would have been a disaster story for a company to have borrowed dollars to finance a sterling-earning project over the same period of time. The same rate movement that gave a welcome 50% discount to the first transaction would have doubled the cost of the initial loan in the second example.

How good is exchange rate forecasting? Clearly, the benefits arising from borrowing 'the right currency at the right time' are considerable, as are the penalties of borrowing the 'wrong currency'. Are there any random walk characteristics in exchange rate movements that might make forecasting difficult? Surveys have been carried out on the accuracy of exchange rate forecasts. Many forecasters' efforts have been less successful in forecasting the direction of movement, let alone the amount of the movement, than would have been expected solely on the basis of chance, that is, their forecasting accuracy would have been improved by relying on the random outcome of the toss of a coin.

A company may also find any windfall profits due to appreciation of the quotation currency against sterling a mixed blessing. The foreign customer is well able to follow exchange rate movements and it is not unknown for customers to press for 'their share' of the windfall in the shape of a retrospective discount on the agreed contract price. Relative market power will then determine who gets precisely what. The customer is not likely to be willing to offer a retrospective increase in the contract price if the exchange rate moves against the supplier.

The exchange risk is exacerbated for contracts that are agreed now but which will only be performed over an extended period of time. The problem remains in a world of fluctuating exchange rates despite the attempts discussed above to bring greater stability into the relative values of currencies.[2]

Incurring costs of production in one currency and revenue to meet those costs in another currency exposes a company to an exchange risk. In a market economy, the existence of a risk generates a provision of cover for that risk.

There are two broad ways in which cover can be purchased against an exchange rate movement. One may buy or sell currency futures contracts, or buy or sell currency forward by buying a forward exchange contract. Thus, there are several ways in which a company or individual may hedge the exchange risk.[3] It is to a discussion of these various instruments that we now turn.

Currency futures contracts

These were among the first contracts traded on the London International Financial Futures Exchange (LIFFE) when it opened in September 1982. They are restricted to the pound sterling, the German mark, the Swiss franc and the Japanese yen. The illustration of the nature and uses of a currency futures contract is restricted to the pound sterling although the general principles apply to the other currencies.[4]

Contracts for multiples of the single contract value of £25,000 are bought and sold for delivery in March, June, September and December of each year. At any one time, three of these dates will be outstanding. Prices are quoted in US dollars per unit of currency, that is, per pound sterling. This is in effect the exchange rate between the two currencies fixed in the contract. See Table 8.1.

Table 8.1 Exchange rates as at 10 November 1983 for the next three delivery dates

Delivery date	LIFFE sterling currency future prices in $US 10.11.1983	% value of the contract
December 1983	1.4910	37,275
March 1984	1.4935	37,337.50
June 1984	1.4965	37,412.50

Source: *LIFFE Weekly Report,* week ending 10 November 1983

Buying say one contract for delivery March 1984 at a price of $1.4935 at this date in November 1983 would mean that the purchaser would receive the following March the sum of £25,000 for which he would have to pay 25,000 × $1.4935 = $37,337.50. Such a contract would act as a hedge for an exporter who knows that he is going to receive the dollar sum and who wishes to know precisely now what the sterling equivalent would be. If he needs not pounds but dollars because he has a known future obligation to pay a dollar sum, then selling a contract means that he has sold £25,000 for a fixed dollar amount and thus secured the exchange rate now for the transaction that will take place on the indicated delivery day. Thus, these contracts may be used by those who need to hedge payments in either of the two currencies.

How did the hedge perform?
Looking forward from the contract date in November 1983 to march 1984, we see that the prevailing spot rate was $1.4425 = £1. thus,

using such a contract to hedge the sterling value of known expected dollar receipts would not have proved as effective as not hedging and bearing the exchange risk oneself. The reader should verify that the advantage of simply bearing the exchange risk oneself would have been per contract £25,000(1.4935 – 1.4425) = £1,275. Hedging the dollar value of £25,000 would have meant the corresponding gain to the hedger. The hedge in this case would have produced the $37,337.50 compared to the 25,000 $1.4425 = $36,062.50 produced by waiting until March 1984 and buying dollars at the then prevailing spot rate of exchange.

The importance of this is to stress that the hedging use of such contracts is to produce certainty in an uncertain world. Leaving the outcome to the vagaries of the market (doing without a hedge and assuming the risk oneself) may or may not produce an outcome that is better than the result from hedging the contract value by buying or selling one of these currency futures contracts. The hedger is buying certainty, not a guarantee that he will get the best possible financial outcome of all possibilities.

Disadvantages of futures contracts as hedges

Perhaps the major disadvantage of these contracts as hedges is that they are standard contracts. They deal in fixed quantities of currency with delivery taking place four times a year. A company seeking a hedge against an unfavourable movement in exchange rates may typically be looking for cover for a particular sum of money at a particular point of time. A multiple of £25,000 delivered in March, June, September of December may simply not be convenient. Such requirements are better met by the tailor-made, non-standard contracts offered to importers and exporters largely by the commercial banks as contracts for the forward exchange of currencies at rates set now.

The standard contracts for currency purchases and sales offered on LIFFE are suitable for trading, that is, they may not be held until delivery is due but the contract itself may be sold for whatever the current rate is by the present holder of the contract. Standard contracts are a prerequisite for trading on an organised market and, as such, are of interest to those who form a view about the trend over time in the prices of these contracts and who buy or sell based on the view they have about the relationship between the current price and the way the price is expected to move in the future. In November 1983, March 1984 Sterling Currency Futures were quoted on LIFFE at $1.4935. If a trader forms a view that this price is likely to move to say $1.50, then he may back this view by buying sterling futures with a view to selling and taking the profit resulting from the price rise. In other words, such contracts are of interest to speculators.

For an 'ordinary' exporter or importer, these contracts present problems that reduce their attractiveness as hedges for the exchange risks inherent in their foreign contracts for the purchase and sale of goods and services.

The currency futures contracts have only four delivery dates per year and are for fixed multiples of £25,000, that is, they are standard contracts, not purpose designed as one-offs to suit the particular requirements of those who face exchange risks in the normal course of their business. The very nature of a standard contract that makes possible a market for the futures contracts themselves makes them less suitable in many situations as hedging instruments.

For an exporter or importer seeking protection against exchange risks for a specific sum of money due to be received or paid at a specific point of time in the future, it is probably more convenient in many cases to seek a specific non-standard contract tailor made for the sums they wish to protect over the periods of time for which they need the protection. This will involve a forward exchange contract through the banking system.

The forward exchange contract

A buyer or seller of foreign currency may not find his needs best met by a standardised contract such as those discussed above. He may wish to guarantee the sterling equivalent of a particular sum of foreign currency expected around a particular date in the future. He may also expect to have to pay a certain amount of foreign exchange at a date in the future and wish to know now what the corresponding sterling payment will be.

If a sum of foreign currency is expected in say 3 months' time and the company is unwilling to bear the exchange risk, then it may sell the expected receipts forward to the bank at a 'forward rate of exchange agreed now'. It may well contact its bank for a forward rate quotation before quoting its foreign customer in his own currency for the export order. An importer may be quoted in the domestic currency of his foreign supplier but needs to be certain of the sterling cost of the goods he is buying in order to more accurately do his own costings. Again, he may contract now with his bank to 'buy the foreign currency forward' that he will need to pay his foreign supplier. He will be quoted a rate for the forward purchase of the required sum of foreign exchange. It brings certainty into his world and eliminates the exchange risks that he is unwilling to bear and unable to forecast–he buys these forward exchange contracts as hedges against the risk of unfavourable movements in exchange rates between now and when he will either have to buy foreign currency to pay his import bills or sell the foreign currency resulting from export orders.

A guide to the rates of exchange may be found from the information published in the financial press. Table 8.2 relates to spot and forward rates prevailing at the close of business on 10 December 1984.

Table 8.2   The pound sterling – spot and forward against the US dollar

Spot closing prices	One month	p.a.	Three months	% pa
1.2025–1.2035	0.03 – 0.06 cents premium	0.45%	0.10–0.05 cents premium	0.25

Source: *Financial Times*, 10 December 1984

The spot rate is the rate for delivery normally two working days hence. If the currency is ordered on say Wednesday, then the spot rate would refer to delivery on the following Friday. It should be realised that these rates are not the rates one would be quoted by one's bank. They are rates for very large sums of money and would only be relevant for multi-million pound transactions. They are, however, a guide to the general level of rates prevailing and to the relationships between the spot and various forward rates.

The premium or discount shown links the spot rate to the quoted forward rates. It applies to the dollar and therefore needs to be deducted in the case of a premium or added in the case of a discount. This is just the opposite to what is suggested by the everyday meaning of the words.

If the spot rate is \$1.2025 = £1, with a one month premium of

0.06 cents, then the 2-month forward rate is $(1.2025 - 0.06) = $1.1425 = £1. It is the dollar that stands at the indicated premium, that is, pounds are cheaper in terms of the dollar by the amount of the premium. pounds for delivery 3 months hence are slightly cheaper still as the average 3-month premium of 0.025 cents is slightly higher than the average 2-month premium of 0.015 cents. A not unreasonable interpretation of this is that, after a long period of decline from around $2.4 = £1 to around $1.2 = £1, the decline has bottomed out and no further significant decline is expected certainly over the next 3 months from the date of the table.

Calculation of the premium as a percentage
The 1 month premium is shown as 0.45% per annum. The middle 1-month premium is $0.5(0.06 - 0.03) = 0.045$ cents per month. This is equal to a per annum rate of $0.045c \times 12 = 0.54$.

This is then expressed as a percentage of the middle closing price of $1.2030. Thus, $(0.54c \times 100)/120.30c = 0.45\%$, quoted in the table as the one month premium.

This is very much a summary statistic, the middle premium expressed as an annual precentage on the middle closing price. rates and associated premiums and discounts are of course continuously fluctuating. A look at the annual rate of premium or discount on 1-month and 3-months money is an indication of how the market expects rates to move over these periods of time. Very high rates of premium would suggest large movements are expected, whereas a set of uniformly small percentages would suggest that no great stresses and strains are present in the foreign exchange market that are thought likely to have significant effects on rates of exchange over the next one or three months.

These rates are 'wholesale' rates. They would be attainable only for very large transactions. It would also be noted that the quoted spot rate is really a 2-day forward rate. Rates for delivery today would be different again. Thus, they are only a guide to the individual who needs to fix a rate now for his own export or import finance needs. He can assume that rates obtainable through his bank will not be as favourable as these forward published rates.

The forward contract with the bank can be tailored to the precise requirements of the customer. He can fix a rate now for a given sum at a given point of time in the future. These are not standard contracts. Each contract is particular in its terms to the individual or company that negotiates such cover through his bank. Nor is the availability of such forward cover limited to 1 and 3 months. Cover for much longer periods of time can be negotiated. Naturally, the longer the period of time for which cover is required, the greater is the cost. The cover is most needed when rates of exchange are fluctuating most violently and it is precisely in these situations that it will be most expensive. It is rather like other forms of insurance in this respect: when it is most needed it costs the most, and when least needed it is available at its cheapest.

We have considered so far in this chapter only examples drawn from the exchange rate between the pound sterling and the United states dollar. For foreign exchange transactions between the UK and the USA this is sufficient. Likewise, if we are concerned with financing trade between any two countries, the exchange rate between those two countries' currencies is what we have to concern ourselves with.

However, although the United States dollar remains an extremely important currency in the world economy, it has declined in relative importance over the last 30 years. As far as the UK is concerned, the Federal Republic of Germany is our major export market and nearly 50% of our export trade goes to countries of the European Economic Community. Thus, many currencies other

Table 8.3

Country	% of UK foreign trade = weight	Change between two points of time between sterling and the individual foreign currency (%)	Contribution to the weighted average = weight × exchange rate (%)
A	50	− 5	−2.5
B	30	+20	+6.0
C	20	+15	+3.0
	Weighted averaged change =		+6.5

Note: if the previous level of the index of such trade-weighted changes stood at 100, then the new level would be 106.5

than the dollar are of vital trade importance to the UK. Some measurement of changes in the value of sterling in relationship to the currencies of trading partners is thus desirable. We need a weighted average change in the value of sterling in relationship to these currencies with the weights chosen to reflect the trade importance of each currency to the UK.

The principles involved in constructing such a trade-weighted index are identical in nature to those already discussed in relationship to the construction of the indices earlier in the book. Table 8.3 illustrates the principles underlying the construction of such an index. It is restricted to three countries to illustrate the principles at work.

The Sterling Index

The system of monetary arrangements since the Second World War, established at the Bretton Woods conference in 1944, envisaged a world of fixed exchange rates, altered rather infrequently as fundamental disequilibria arose. This system broke down in the early 1970s and was replaced by a world in which exchange rates were to be much more free to move than had previously been the case. Typically, this means any one currency rising in value against certain currencies and falling in value against other currencies. thus, some measurement of an average change against a basket of currencies is intuitively more desirable in this situation than simply quoting bilateral currency exchange rates between sterling and a list of other currencies separately.

From previous discussions on indices such as the Retail Prices Index and the FTSE 100 Share Index, it should be clear that a weighted index is indicated. This follows from recognition that not all countries are equally important either in the size of their domestic economies or the importance for the world economy of their foreign trade.

The weights for the Sterling Index were calculated for 18 countries by the International Monetary Fund using a multiple exchange rate model (MERM).[5] Thus, any one currency's appreciation or depreciation is shown as a weighted average change against the other currencies.

The MERM produces a set of weights for each of the 18

Table 8.4 Sterling Index

Currency	Weights 1977 trade flows MERM model	Exchange rates with sterling 8.1.1985	Exchange rates with sterling 14.1.1985	Unweighted change $= \dfrac{(4)-(3)}{(3)} \times 100$	Weighted change $= (2) \times (5)$ %
(1)	(2)	(3)	(4)		
1 US dollar	0.2463	1.1475	1.1105	-3.2244	-0.7942
2 W. German mark	0.1408	3.6150	3.5450	-1.9364.	-0.2726
3 Japanese yen	0.1367	290.2500	283.2500	-2.4117	-0.3297
4 French franc	0.1039	11.1450	10.8400	-2.7367	-0.2843
5 Italian lira	0.0718	2223.2500	2171.0000	-2.3502	-0.1687
6 Dutch guilder	0.0480	4.0825	4.0000	-2.0208	-0.0970
7 Irish punt	0.0405	1.1605	1.1390	-1.8526	-0.0750
8 Belgian franc	0.0404	72.3500	70.8500	-2.0733	-0.0838
9 Swedish krone	0.0373	10.3600	10.1125	-2.3889	-0.0891
10 Swiss franc	0.0300	3.0200	2.9650	-1.8212	-0.0546
11 Norwegian krone	0.0211	10.4625	10.2250	-2.2700	-0.0479
12 Australian dollar	0.0199	1.4160	1.3745	-2.9308	-0.0583
13 Spanish peseta	0.0186	199.2500	194.7000	-2.2836	-0.0425
14 Canadian dollar	0.0151	1.5165	1.4690	-3.1322	-0.0473
15 Danish krone	0.0109	12.9400	12.6600	-2.1638	-0.0236
16 Austrian schilling	0.0100	25.4500	24.8300	-2.4361	-0.0244
17 Finish markka	0.0085	7.5795	7.4310	-1.9592	-0.0167

Change in the Effective Rate Index from
8.1.1985 to 14.1.1985 =   -2.5097%

Note: At close (4.00 pm) on 8.1.1985, the ERI stood at 72.7 (1975=100)' The decline of 2.5097% by the close on 14.1.1985 therefore took the ERI: to a new low of 72.7 - 1.8246 = 70.87

countries, enabling 18 Effective Exchange Rates to be calculated as a weighted average of the remaining 17 currencies' exchange values. naturally, greater prominence is given in the UK media to the Sterling Index.[6] A worked example of the Sterling ERI is set out in table 8.4. The principle underlying the weights is fairly simple but is more complex than the simple introductory example above.[7]

From the currencies listed, a large number of combinations can be envisaged that would cause the UK's trade balance to change by the same amount as a 1% change in sterling against each of the other currencies. The weights are chosen to ensure that this results in a 1% change in the index.

This may be put another way. A 1% change in the value of sterling against each of the 17 currencies simultaneously would produce a 1% change in the index. This follows from the nature of the index as a weighted arithmetic mean with the sum of the weights equal to unity. A large number of other changes in rates of exchange are also estimated to change the trade balance by 1%. the weights are then such that each of these other possible changes having this effect on the trade balance also change the index by 1%.

Weights quantify for the purposes of statistical calculations what is often qualitatively obvious. The dollar weight of 0.2463 shows that a 1% change in the $/£ exchange rate would have almost one-quarter of 1% effect on the UK trade balance but only one-twentieth of 1% effect on the US trade balance (weight = 0.0506).

In other words, the US dollar is more important to UK trade than the UK pound is to US trade. This conclusion is not obvious from export figures alone. In 1982, exports to the United States totalled £7,457m and imports from the United States amounted to £6,638m. trade flows alone would have resulted in weights much more nearly identical. The weights derived from the model used reflect the impact of many more variables and their interactions both within the countries that are engaged in trade and between them in international markets.

The Sterling Index thus calculates the change in the value of sterling against the 17 other currencies of this particluar basket as a weighted arithmetic mean. Its arithmetic form is thus similar to that of the Retail Price Index and the FTSE 100 Share Index. Much of the comment in Chapters 2 and 3 will therefore apply to the Sterling Index.

The presentation of the index in the financial publications of the Central Statistical Office and the media generally takes the form of an index number related to a base of 100 as at January 1975. The weighted average calculated change is converted into an index point change in the manner already reviewed for previous indices. It is published at 8.30 a.m. each working day and then hourly from 9.00 a.m. to 4.00 p.m.

At the 4.00 p.m. closing on 8 January 1985, the index stood at 72.7.[8] This means that over the 10 years since the base was established, the average decline in the value of sterling against this currency basket has been (100 - 72.7) = 27.3%. Approximately one-quarter of this decline has been due to the decline of the pound against the dollar.

Significance of the Sterling Index

Changes in the Sterling Index are simply changes in the weighted arithmetic mean value of sterling against the other currencies in the basket. For whom and for what purposes is this particular index useful?

It is part of the whole array of statistics measuring various aspects of our economic life that have appeared over the years. It provides information of a quantitative nature on how sterling is varying in value in relationship to other currencies. It is unwise to regard either an increase or decrease in the relative value of a currency as necessarily 'good' or 'bad' in any sense of these emotive words. Fluctuating exchange rates have an important role to play in the economy. A relative decline in the exchange value of a currency has an important corrective function as part of the response of the economic system to a balance of payments deficit as does an appreciation of a currency in situations of a balance of payments surplus. On the other hand, the index will move in response to speculative buying or selling of currency or in response to interest rate differences between financial centres. Thus, movements in the index may reflect any combination of a number of different factors. Movements in the index are not self-explanatory and alone have very little significance: what is more interesting and revealing is the explanation for any particular movement.

If a manufacturer exports to and imports from this particular group of countries in proportions closely allied to the weights of the index, then the index may tell him something about the average currency impact of the exchange rate changes. In practice, any international trading company is likely to find that monitoring the exchange rate movements of its own markets is likely to be more informative.

Sharp increases in exports to the United States have been noticed by many commentators,[9] in particular, a 25% increase between 1983 and 1984. It would be wrong to attribute this entirely to the 50% decline in the value of sterling between 1982 and 1984 without careful analysis.

British exporters have been criticised[10] for devoting their sales forces to export markets during a recession and neglecting them again when the domestic recession is over. It is thus debatable what proportion of this increase in exports is to be attributed to the exchange rate movement and how much to the coincident recession at home.

General Interpretation of the Sterling Index

Changes in the Sterling Index need to be carefully considered. Certainly, the reader should hesitate before accepting any simplistic interpretation of the causes and meaning of changes in the index.

Any changes that take place in the index by definition imply that the previous level of the index represented a disequilibrium in some sense in the individual exchange rates.

At any one time, there will be special factors influencing the demand for individual currencies. In early 1985, the relatively high demand for US dollars was due to relatively high United States interest rates. By January 1987, the demand for dollars had fallen because of fears about the impact of the US balance of payments deficit on exchange rates and the influence of the record budget deficit on possible future inflation rates. The falling price of oil until late 1986 depressed the demand for sterling. This recovered following the success of OPEC in raising the price of oil from around $12 to $18 per barrel. The state of industrial relations as perceived in various countries influences the relative attractiveness of their currencies. The miners' strike in Britain in 1985 and problems highlighted by demonstrating students in Paris in 1987 are examples of events influencing the foreign exchange markets of the world.[11]

At any other time, there will be another story to be told that will account for the particular changes being recorded in the index. The

reader should beware of any emotional interpretation of movements in the index. He should eschew completely ideas that any
movements are necessarily good or bad.

Movements in the index send different signals to different groups.
A fall in the index is likely to be welcomed by exporters rather than
importers and vice versa for a rise in the index. Those with foreign
currency denominated bank balances will be much more interested
in the individual exchange rates between sterling and the currency
of denomination of their bank accounts. In these cases, simple
unweighted individual exchange rates are likely to be more
informative than the index.

As far as general economic policy is concerned, any government
is likely to become concerned if the index is judged to be falling too
far and too fast. It will worry about the inflation consequences of
such a prolonged fall. The government may also worry about a
prolonged rise in the index, especially if this follows 'advice' from
pressure groups that the 'high rate' is making exporting difficult and
adversely affecting employment in export-oriented industries.
These are all questions of balance and judgement.

The Special Drawing Right unit

There are two major basket units quoted regularly in the financial
press, the European Currency Unit (ECU) and the Special Drawing
Right (SDR). The former, reviewed in Chapter 4, is the unit of
account of the European Economic Community and lies at the heart
of the European Monetary System and has already been discussed
in detail. The SDR is the unit of account of the International
Monetary Fund and is discussed below. The reader will note that
the broad considerations applying to the ECU also apply to the
SDR although the detail is vastly different.

The present unit dates from 1 January 1986 and may be reviewed
every 5 years. Therefore, the composition shown in Table 8.5 may
change as from 1 January 1991.

The SDR is composed of the five currencies listed in column (1)
with the amounts of each currency as shown in column (2). The
currencies are those of the 'Group of Five', that is, the five most
important industrial nations that are members of the International
Monetary Fund.

The five countries were chosen from the membership of the Fund

Table 8.5 Composition of the Special Drawing Right unit

Currency	Amounts of the national currencies in the SDR basket	Weights on 1.1.1986 (%)
(1)	(2)	(3)
US dollar	0.452	42
German mark	0.527	19
French franc	1.020	12
Japanese yen	33.400	15
Pound sterling	0.0893	12
		100

Source: IMF, Washington

on the basis of export performance plus the currencies officially held in the Fund. The five are thus those countries with the largest exports of goods and services during the period 1980 to 1984 together with currency balances officially held on average during the same period.

The United States was responsible for 42% of the total for the five top countries. In second place was Germany with 19%, Japan 15%, France and the United Kingdom with 12% each. These percentage shares then form the weights of the SDR unit. 'They broadly reflect the relative importance of these currencies in international trade and finance.'[12]

Of the SDR unit 42% is to consist of the United States dollar. But how many dollars should this be? How many German marks should represent 19% of the basket, and so on for the other currencies? The method chosen to answer these questions involves linking the current SDR to values of the predecessor in use until 31 December 1985. The specific amounts of each currency in the basket are derived on the basis of the average of the daily noon values of the SDR for the period from 1 October to 31 December inclusive. These values were taken from the London foreign exchange market.[13]

This average dollar value was $1.07619. Thus 42% of this is the

$0.452 in the SDR unit introduced on 1 January 1986. The dollar value of 19% of this average value of the unit is then converted into marks at the average value of the mark in terms of the dollar for the same period and comes to the 0.527 DM in the revised unit. A similar calculation for the yen, french franc and pound sterling enabled column (2) of the table to be completed.

As for the ECU, the weights change over time as exchange rates move. The unit contains 0.452 dollars. The value of the unit on 23 January 1987 was $1.2664. The weight of the dollar in the SDR basket on this date was thus $(0.452/1.2664)100 = 35.69\%$. It has thus depreciated against the SDR in just over a year from its original weight of 42% by some 15%. This is just one consequence of the economic problems of the United States arising from its record balance of payments deficit in the early months of 1987.

Uses of the SDR unit

The SDR unit is the unit of account of the International Monetary Fund. The IMF dates from the Bretton Woods Conference in 1944. The anxiety at that time, as now, was that a means should be created to prevent countries with balance of payments deficits attempting to deal with them in a way that would spread unemployment throughout the world economy.

Countries with balance of payments difficulties are likely to introduce remedial action that includes restrictions on imports by imposing quotes and tariffs. Such restrictions on trade then create unemployment elsewhere in the world. Retaliation can then result in a downward spiral of rising unemployment, falling output and declining trade. This was the experience of the 1930s. The view in 1944 was that a new world trade policy was necessary to minimise the possibility of a return to these conditions.

The alternative to balance of payments policies involving restrictions on trade includes creating funds that can be lent to countries with payment problems. This will enable them to finance their deficits and give time for necessary internal policies to be adopted and take effect. In the interim, the lending will avoid the need for short-term panic action that would tend to spread recession and unemployment around the world.

The funds that the IMF has for such lending are denominated in SDRs although they are subscribed in the national currencies of the member states. The IMF makes SDRs available by selling them to members in exchange for their own currencies. Thus, lending changes the composition but not the overall size of the Fund's reserves.[14]

Although the lending of SDRs does not formally increase the means of settling debts in world trade, the quality of world liquidity is markedly enhanced. Payment for SDRs in the form of a member state's own currency may mean that the IMF is accepting a currency that has virtually no role in world trade and lending in return the currencies of the five major industrial nations of the world. It is not, of course, always the 'rich' lending to the 'poor'. Wealthy nations can and do get into difficulties and borrow form the fund.

It should not be assumed that because the unit is called the Special Drawing Right that countries may in all circumstances borrow at their own discretion just as and when they feel like running a larger trade deficit than would otherwise be possible.

An ongoing debate concerns the criteria that the Fund imposes on would-be borrowers, the so-called conditionality. This refers to the requirement that the IMF lays down on members wishing to borrow. The Fund may exert quite detailed requirements as to domestic economic policies to be followed as a condition of granting a loan denominated in SDR units.[14]

The Fund comes under a certain amount of pressure especially from debtor countries to increase the supply of SDRs to provide balance of payments finance.[15],[16]

It has been argued that such an increase would help developing nations to finance the capital imports required for economic growth and at the same time provide orders to maintain employment in the capital goods industries of the developed world, a symbiosis of interest. Opponents of these proposals feel that the inflationary consequences would be unacceptable and attention would be diverted away from sound domestic monetary and fiscal policies.

Pressure also comes from within the IMF for an increase in the availability of SDRs.[17] As the SDR is a basket unit, increases can only come about if the five members, whose currencies make up the basket, are prepared to increase the input of their individual national currencies into the IMF. The national governments of the five thus have to agree in effect to transfer their own resources to developing countries if an increase in SDRs is to take place. Thus, quota reviews are made regularly but are not always accepted.[18] SDRs can only be made up from supplies of national currencies in proportion to their representation in the unit. Purchasing power of the SDR is thus linked to the purchasing powers of the national currencies that make up the unit.

Some commentators would like the IMF to have the power to print SDRs, in other words, to make the SDR a pure fiat money. There are several objections to this, both theoretical and practical, that are likely to ensure that the SDR does not develop in this direction.

It would mean national states surrendering control over the payments medium to a bureaucracy of over 100 member states of the IMF nearly all of whom have conflicting interests. It is hard to imagine the domestic control techniques of open market operations and discounting being transferred to this supra-national body.

Interest rates

There are two interest rates on SDRs, the official and the market-determined. It is the latter that are generally printed in the financial press.

Members of the IMF contribute SDRs in the form of their national currencies and may borrow SDRs from the Fund. If more has been borrowed than contributed, then interest is paid to the Fund. If more has been contributed than borrowed, then there is a net interest payment by the Fund to the member state.

These official rates are settled quarterly in advance. They have many of the qualities of 'administered prices', that is, prices fixed by an essentially arbitrary formula. Movements in interest rates in the five states reflecting market forces and policy decisions do filter through to have an effect on the quarterly revision of the SDR official interest rate. An individual country's rate determines the SDR official rate in proportion to the amount of the currency in the basket and the level of the chosen representative rate.[20]

The published SDR rates in the financial press are not normally these official rates but market rates for non-official uses. They are much closer to Eurocurrency rates. This should not be really surprising as SDR deposits need to be competitive with other alternative instruments. These other non-official uses include the use of the SDR as the denominator of bond issues, certificates of deposit and certain bank loans.

The attraction of any basket currency lies largely in its use as a hedge in a world of exchange-rate volatility. If exchange rates of the five constituent currencies move in opposite directions, the value of the SDR unit will tend to be preserved.

At the time of writing, both the SDR and the ECU units are finding private as well as their original official uses but the ECU is increasing its penetration of private sector transactions at a faster rate than the SDR.

The Introduction of the SDR

The SDR was designed specifically to 'meet the need . . . for a supplement to existing reserve assets'.[21] Thus, it was intended to enable countries to finance balance of payments deficits if their existing reserves of foreign currencies and gold were inadequate.

In the discussion on the creation of the Eurocurrencies Market, emphasis was placed on the consequences of the lending of surplus countries to those needing to borrow to finance the counterpart deficits. Spectacular examples of this include the huge claims being built up by the large surpluses of the oil-exporting countries following the rapid and substantial oil price increases of the late 1970s. Although this was reversed somewhat by the collapse of oil prices in the 1980s, there still remains a major balance of payments problem for developing countries due very largely to the level of energy import prices. Thus, in part, the forces at work leading to growth in Eurocurrency deposits were also creating pressure for the wider use of the SDR.

World trade has been helped by the trade deficits of the United States. These deficits are met by a willingness around the world to hold the dollar. Pressure for an enhanced role for the SDR fades somewhat when the supply of dollars from US deficits increases. This was the situation in the 1960s when the United States ran large deficits associated with its Vietnam War expenditure. The return to surplus of the United States balance of payments during 1968–9 caused a capital inflow which in its turn caused a decline in the dollar reserves of other countries. Pressure to offset this loss to the reserves led to the first allocation of SDRs in 1969.[22]

Pressure has been eased again in the 1980s with a return to large US trade deficits.

Table 8.6 illustrates how little progress there has been in the growth of the use of SDRs as a reserve generally. Although the amount of SDRs just about doubled in the decade, SDRs as a percentage of total world reserves actually fell to just 2.5% of the

Table 8.6 Official holdings of reserve assets (in billions of SDR)

	1973	% of total	1983	% of total
Reserve positions in the IMF	6.2	2.9	29.4	4.2
SDRs	8.8	4.1	17.5	2.5
Foreign exchange including ECUs	102.7	48.3	293.3	41.6
Gold	95.0	44.7	364.1	51.7
Total	212.7	100.0	704.3	100.0

Source: International Monetary Fund Annual Report, 1983, Table 14

total by 1983. Foreign exchange holdings and gold remained overwhelmingly the most important form of official reserve assets throughout the period. Some 70% of the worlds's foreign exchange reserves consist of United States dollars.[23]

There is an interesting contrast in the world economy. In the discussion of Eurocurrencies, it was stated that demand for Eurocurrency loans came very strongly from countries borrowing to finance their balance of payments deficits. The United States has for many years run large external deficits but has been able to finance them by foreigners' willingness to hold dollars. Thus, the US deficits have provided the wherewithal to finance the deficits of other countries.

A decreased willingness of the commercial banks to finance the current account deficits of Third World countries on the same scale as before because of the problems of default and rescheduling is likely to lead to further pressure on the IMF to increase the flow of SDR finance for such purposes.

The implication that the problems of the balance of payments finance of these countries can easily be solved by an increase in the availability of SDRs is a gross oversimplification. As Chapter 4 on Eurocurrencies has shown, the deficits involve a transfer of resources from the countries enjoying balance of payments surpluses.

The role of the International Monetary Fund is not that of a development aid giver; it is essentially a monetary institution lending short-term for balance of payments problems. It is analogous to a bank in that its reserves contributed by the members may be withdrawn if needed by the members. This is akin to an ordinary commercial bank's readiness to repay its depositors on demand. It also has similar responsibilities of stewardship and a duty to ensure repayment of loans on time–again a direct analogy with commercial bank lending is apparent here.

Although hopes have been nurtured in some quarters that the SDR would replace foreign currency reserves, this has not happened. There have, however, been significant changes in the foreign exchange components of these reserves. The relative importance of the United States dollar has declined and that of the German mark the Japanese yen and the Swiss franc increased. As the table shows, national currencies and gold have dominated countries' reserve assets over the 15 years or so since the introduction of the SDR and look likely to do so for the foreseeable future.

Notes

1 Commons Public Accounts Committee, Select Committee on Industry and Trade, reported in the *Sunday Express*, 27 March 1983.

2 See Chapter 4 above.

3 Hedging is an operation undertaken to protect oneself against price movements over which one has no control and which one is either unable or unwilling to forecast.

4 London International Financial Futures Exchange *Summary of Contracts* for details of this and the other currency contracts traded.

5 For the complete set of weights derived from the MERM model of the IMF, see *Bank of England Quarterly Bulletin*, Vol. 21, March 1981, p. 70.

6 Published regularly in Central Statistical Office *Economic Trends* and *Financial Statistics*. Published daily in the *Financial Times* and other financial publications.

7 The model used to calculate a set of weights that satisfy the criteria discussed above is a set of simultaneous equations. It involves rather complex econometrics and the interested reader is referred to
J. R. Artis, and R. R. Romberg, 'A multilateral exchange rate model', *IMF Staff Papers*, Vol. 20, No. 3, November 1973.

Additional comment is to be found in: UK Treasury, *Economic Progress Report*, No. 130, February 1981. UK Treasury, *Economic Progress Report*, No. 172, October 1984. 'Revision to the calculation of effective exchange rates', *Bank of England Quarterly Bulletin*, Vol. 21, No. 1, March 1981, pp. 69–70.

8   *Financial Times*, 9 January 1985, p. 25.

9   T. Wilkinson, 'British exports riding high on the dollar', *Sunday Telegraph*, 30 September 1984.

10 D. Connell, *The United Kingdom's Performance in Export Markets*, NEDO Books, 1980.

11 The miners' strike was a particular factor of influence when this chapter was initially written. By May 1986, fear of terrorism had depressed the demand for sterling by American tourists. At any given time, there are always special transient factors of importance as well as longer-run factors such as persistent differences in inflation rates. By January 1987, the size of the United States balance of payments deficit was depressing the demand for dollars.

12 International Monetary Fund, *International Financial Statistics*, December 1986, p. 7.

13 International Monetary Fund, *IFS Supplement on Exchange Rates*, No. 9, 1985, p. v. Exchange rates from the London foreign exchange market are used. If the London market is closed, then New York noon rates are used. If both are closed, then rates from the Frankfurt market are the third choice.

14 'Is the IMF too strict?' *Lloyds Bank International Financial Outlook*, No. 15, June 1983.

15 J. Williamson, *A New SDR Allocation*, Institute for International Economics, MIT Press, Cambridge, Mass.

16 J. Williamson, 'It's time for the IMF to use its power to help debtors', 'Financial Guardian', *Guardian*, 4 April 1983.

17 Summary Proceedings, Annual Meeting of the IMF, 1983. Presentation of the Thirty-Eighth Annual Report. J. de Larosiere, Chairman of the Executive Board and Managing Director of the IMF, p. 29.

18 The United States Congress was particularly reluctant to accept the Eighth Review of Quotas in 1983.

19 R. I. McKinnon, *Money in International Exchanges; The Convertible Currency System*, pp. 281–2, Oxford University Press.

20 The representative rates vary. The dollar rate is the 3-month Treasury Bill yield. This was 5.39% on 23 January 1987. The dollar value of the SDR was $1.2664. There are 45.2c in the SDR unit. The contribution of the US dollar to the official interest rate on the unit would therefore be $(0.452 \times 5.39/1.2664)\% = 1.924\%$.

The German rate is a 3-month inter-bank deposit rate, the French rate a 3-month inter-bank rate against private paper, the Japanese rate a 2-month rate on private bills, and the UK rate is a 3-month yield on treasury bills.

The contributions of each of these rates to the official SDR rate is then calculated as for the dollar above. The sum of the individual contributions is then the official interest rate for the next quarter.

21 L. P. Thompson-McCausland, 'The place of Special drawing rights in the international monetary system', *Bank of England Quarterly Bulletin*, Vol. 8, No. 2, June 1968.

22 P. B. Kenen, 'Use of the SDR to Supplement or Substitute for other Means of Finance', *Reprints in International Finance*, No. 23, December 1983, Princeton University, Princeton, NJ.

23 Governor of the Bank of England, 'The role and future of the international financial institutions', *Bank of England Quarterly Bulletin*, Vol. 24, No. 4, December 1984.

Chapter Nine

The Eurocurrencies market

A Eurocurrency is any currency held outside its country of origin. Thus, United States dollars, held on deposit in London, are one example of a Eurocurrency deposit. The term is potentially misleading. The 'Euro' refers to the early development of the market in Europe and in London in particular and not to the countries of origin of the currencies. Thus, on this definition, any currency could be a Eurocurrency. Although the United States dollar is quantitatively the most significant of the Eurocurrencies, other important Eurocurrencies include sterling, the German mark, the French franc, the Swiss franc, the Canadian dollar, the Italian lira and the Japanese yen. This list is by no means exhaustive and many other currency deposit rates are regularly quoted in the financial press data on the Eurocurrencies market.

How a Eurocurrency deposit arises

These deposits arise as a result of balance of payments surpluses and deficits. They are thus the result of imbalances in trade flows between countries.

A country with a balance of payments surplus, one that is exporting more than it is importing, acquires ownership of foreign currency denominated deposits. A simple example will illustrate.

If a country exports goods and services worth £10,000,000,000 and imports £9,000,000,000, then foreign currency payments made in settlement of its import bill will be £9bn but receipts for its exports will total £10bn. Its financial institutions will thus have acquired £1bn of foreign currency denominated deposits. Thus, as by definition, a Eurocurrency deposit is a deposit in a country outside its country of origin, balance of payments surpluses lead to the creation of these deposits.

Consider next a country with a balance of payments deficit–importing more than it is exporting. It has a problem of how to finance the deficit. In a two-country world, the counterpart deficit of the above surplus of £1bn would leave the deficit partner in trade with a financing problem also of £1bn.

Thus, surplus countries or rather their financial institutions acquire Eurocurrency deposits and deficit countries seek to borrow in this market to finance their deficits.

Owing to imbalances in world trade, countries have tended to be in persistent surplus or deficit. Thus, the Eurocurrencies 'pool' has been constantly supplied with deposits by surplus countries and has been equally readily drained by persistent deficit countries eager to borrow.

Thus, it is easy to see that the necessary condition for continued growth of the Eurocurrencies market is that deficits and surpluses should be a permanent feature of the world economy. The financial institutions in this market can be thought of as acting as intermediaries, taking deposits from institutions in surplus countries and lending them to borrowers in deficit countries.

If the present pattern of surpluses and deficits continues, then Eurocurrencies will continue to pile up and financial institutions will seek lending outlets which, in the main, will continue to be the deficit countries.

Difficulties with Eurocurrency loan repayments is one of the main reasons behind the pressure referred to in Chapter 8 by and on the IMF to increase SDR quotas, that is, provide another means by which Less Developed Countries can continue to finance their deficits.

One way of looking at the net result of this system in operation is to see it as a means whereby countries which produce more than they consume finance the excess consumption of deficit countries which consume more than they produce. In some respects, this system may be seen as transferring resources from the developed to the developing world.

How banks protect themselves

Clearly, a bank experiencing default on loans previously made may seek to reduce its involvement in future loans to that particular client, be he an individual, an institution or a country. There is some evidence in 1987 that this is happening. It may also increase its bad debts provision in its annual accounts.

Banks may seek to protect themselves by means of syndicated loans and floating rate loans.[1] Reference to these appear in the financial press.

The syndicated loan is simply a loan put together by contributions from a number of participating banks. Thus, if the borrower defaults, any one bank is at risk only to the extent of the fraction of the loan that it has subscribed. Thus, it is not uncommon to see advertised in the press a multi-million pound equivalent Eurocurrency loan to a country with balance of payments difficulties with the names of several merchant and commercial banks contributing to the overall sum raised.

The floating rate loan allows rates of interest charged during the life of the loan to ensure rates move in line with those prevailing in the market generally.

History does have a habit of repeating itself. During the 1931 crisis, international debt defaulters comprised many of the same countries in default today. More prudent application of banking criteria for the assessment of borrowers also seems likely in the future.

It is easy to see why deficit countries should prefer to borrow in this market to finance their payments deficits rather than adopt internal deflationary policies necessary to eliminate the deficit. To borrow means that the country can consume more than it produces, that is, maintain higher living standards than would otherwise be possible.

If the borrowing were used to finance a capital project that would produce foreign exchange earnings to repay the loan with a return in foreign exchange over and above the interest cost and capital sum borrowed, then the deficit would tend to close. However, foreign currency borrowings are not often subject to any such criteria when it is a foreign government that is making application for a loan. They all too often simply add a borrowing debt to the debt total already incurred.

Instability of the market

The instability of such a system is fairly simple to appreciate. Borrowers will have an increasing temptation to default on repayment of capital and interest. The political unacceptability at home of domestic policies designed to reduce balance of payment deficits means that default is easier to contemplate. When the borrower is a sovereign nation state, the lender can have little effective pressure to exert to ensure payment. The same would certainly not be true for an individual commercial borrower in this market. In the latter case, much more careful scrutiny of the proposal for which the loan is to be raised is likely to be made and a defaulting borrower is likely to be much more exposed to the threat of legal action in the case of default.

This system of large Eurocurrency loans to deficit countries is therefore likely to produce a banking crisis if prolonged for long enough on a large enough scale. Although the nation state borrower may default, the bank retains an obligation to repay the depositor at the end of the term for which the money has been deposited.

Borrowing for relatively short periods from depositors and lending relatively long initially to countries that then default so that the lending becomes indefinitely long or is written off as a bad debt or, as it is euphemistically sometimes put, rescheduled lies at the heart of the problem.

There is then the political pressure on the banks to take a 'reasonable line' with incipient or actual defaulters both from Western governments anxious about political developments in defaulting countries as well as directly from the banks' anxiety to protect their own banking operations and interests in debtor countries.

Yet there is no easy way out of this situation. If debtors were to eliminate their deficits, then surplus countries would no longer have surpluses. Historically acquired debts to Eurocurrency lenders would still exist but the supply of such currencies would dry up. Banks would then find it less easy in an emergency to borrow on their own account to repay their debtors.[2]

Eurocurrency interest rates

Despite what has been said above, the Eurocurrency market offers institutional and individual borrowers a range of currencies that are available to be borrowed at widely different interest rates.

Eurocurrency deposit rates depend upon the currency and on the period of time for which the deposit is made. The rate paid is generally higher the longer the period for which the deposit is made, although generally the rate does not vary greatly with the period for which the money is deposited. Although loan rates will vary with the nature of the purpose for which the money is borrowed, the length of time for which it is borrowed and the amount borrowed, loan rates will stand in the same sort of relationship as the deposit rates illustrated in Table 9.1.

Table 9.1 Eurocurrency deposit rates

Currency	3-month deposit	Exchange rate movement 1.1.1975 to 23.1.1985 IMF MERM Model
Sterling	10%–10.125	70.7
US dollar	8–8	146.5
German mark	5½%–5⅝	120.2
Swiss Franc	4–4	135.9
		Base = 100 for all currencies 1.1.1975

Source: *Financial Times*, 9 January 1985

The interest rates paid on Eurocurrency deposits are shown in the table for a few of the major currencies. Notice that it is interest rates that are shown and not prices. Thus, Eurocurrencies are borrowed and lent, not bought and sold.

Raising a Eurocurrency Loan

If a potential borrower is thinking of raising a Eurocurrency loan, which currency should be borrowed? The table simply does not provide enough information to enable a choice to be safely made.

The 'naive' approach to borrowing the currency with the lowest interest rate, namely the Swiss franc with a deposit rate of just

under 5% and hence a relatively low associated borrowing rate, is
certainly not the answer, regardless of the purposes for which the
money is being raised. In other words, it is important to understand
that the spread of rates from around 10% for Eurosterling to 5% for
Swiss francs is much more a sign of an equilibrium relationship
between the currencies than any glaring disequilibrium that will be
closed by a rush to borrow Swiss francs at the expense of borrowing
sterling.

Consider the following projects as examples of the principles
involved in making the decision about which particular Eurocurrency to borrow.

Project One: Borrowing in the Eurocurrencies Market to buy or expand a business in Switzerland

In this example, it might make sense to borrow Swiss francs. As the
business is located in Switzerland and presumably earning its cash
flow in Swiss francs, the earnings will be in the same currency as the
loan. The borrower is therefore protected from any change in the
exchange rate between the cash flow currency and the currency in
which the loan is denominated.

Project Two: Borrowing in the Eurocurrencies Market to buy or expand a business in England supplying the domestic market

In this example, it could be the height of financial folly to borrow
Swiss francs to finance an investment that is to generate a sterling
cash flow. In this case, the currency to be repaid and the cash flow
currency are different. The financial risks now include variations in
the sterling Swiss franc exchange rate.

If the Swiss franc were to appreciate against sterling by the time
repayment is due, this would effectively increase the sterling cost of
the loan and thus lower the return on capital of the forward
projected cash flow made during the initial investment appraisal.

A 5% appreciation of the Swiss franc would be sufficient to wipe
out the apparent initial interest rate advantage of borrowing Swiss
francs instead of Eurosterling. More than a 5% appreciation and
borrowing the 10% sterling would have proved cheaper to borrow
than the 5% Swiss francs.

What is the likelihood of such an appreciation of the Swiss franc
taking place against sterling? Reference to the Sterling Index shows

that sterling fell by 1.8% in just 6 days in January 1985. This in itself would have eroded nearly 2% of the apparent interest advantage of Swiss francs over Eurosterling, nearly 40%.

Interpreting the spread of interest rates

Thus, the spread of Eurocurrency rates of interest is related to the 'strength' or 'weakness' of the national currency unit. A 'strong' currency is one that is likely to appreciate against 'weak' currencies, the latter being those most likely to depreciate.

Sterling is the weakest of the four currencies in Table 9.1 and Euro Swiss francs the strongest. Such ranking in terms of 'strength' and 'weakness' does not change markedly over the years. The stronger a currency in this sense, the lower the interest rate for loan on the Eurocurrencies Market. This is because the effective borrowing cost is increased by the depreciation of the weaker currencies as discussed above. Thus, adjusted for this consideration, the rates would appear much more equal than the apparent discrepancies suggest.

Occasionally, one may read of a local authority 'discovering' how cheaply Swiss francs may be borrowed and suggesting that the council fund its borrowing by raising Swiss franc loans. The folly of such an uninformed suggestion should now be clear in the light of the discussion above.

'Weak' or 'Strong'

The strength of a currency depends principally upon the rate of inflation in the country in question.[1] The higher the rate of inflation relative to other countries, the more the exchange value relative to other countries is likely to fall. Thus, if in countries A and B the inflation rates are 10% and 5% per annum respectively and the exchange rate is initially 1.5A = 1B between their currencies, then the new exchange rate, because of inflation, might be expected to change to $(110/105)1.5 = 1.57A = 1B$, that is, a depreciation in value of currency A relative to B because of the higher rate of inflation in the former. This follows from the purchasing power parity theory.[3] It is not the whole story, but persistent differences in inflation rates are of significant explanatory value in determining long-run trends in relative currency values. The lower rates of inflation in Switzerland and Germany than in the United Kingdom explain a lot of the divergent trends in the effective exchange rates for these currencies. Starting at 100 in 1975, the German mark and Swiss franc have risen in relative value in moving from 100 to 120.2 in the case of the German mark and from 100 to 135.9 in the case of the Swiss franc. The higher rate of inflation in the UK is of major explanatory significance, but is not the whole story, in the fall from 100 to 70.7 over the same period. Whilst inflation played some part in the rise over the same period for the US dollar from 100 to 146.5, other factors such as the level of US interest rates to finance the Federal Deficit were important at this time.

Past history in this sense is taken by the market as a signal as to what to expect in the future and the interest rates on Eurocurrency loans and deposits adjust as discussed above.

Project Three: Borrowing by a country with a balance of payments deficit to finance that deficit

This may typically be a Third World Country seeking, as discussed above, to consume internally more than it produces domestically. It thus imports the balance and seeks to pay for the excess of imports over exports by raising a Eurocurrency loan.[4]

As discussed above, if the money borrowed finances a capital project with foreign exchange earnings potential and the currency of the principal intended export market is borrowed, then few problems may arise if the project is well managed.

The problem arises when the borrowings are used to finance a higher level of domestic consumption than would otherwise be possible. In this case, there is a very much greater likelihood that the borrower will seek rescheduling or default in whole or in part on the capital and/or interest repayments. It may in certain cases go to maintain a corrupt life style for the ruling elite. It is in this area that the threats of instability of the system mainly come.

For the business investor, the Eurocurrencies Market offers yet another possible source of loanable funds which, in certain circumstances, may prove more attractive than other financing alternatives available. Some of the major caveats about borrowing in this market have been looked at above. Naturally, for anyone actually contemplating borrowing in this market, there are very many more points of detail to consider, depending upon the nature of the planned project.

Certificates of deposit

This section on certificates of deposit (CD) is included in the chapter on Eurocurrencies because the CD first arose as a development in the Eurodollar market. It was in 1966 that the First National Bank of America introduced to London the negotiable dollar certificate of deposit.

The Primary CD Market

An investor faces a choice. He may be prepared to deposit say his dollars with a bank outside the United States and to tie them up for a predetermined period of normally up to one year, that is, to make a Eurodollar time deposit. He will only normally be able to withdraw his money at the end of the stated period of time. For this, he will receive a market-determined rate of interest.

He will, however, be illiquid for the period of the deposit. If, instead, he obtains a certificate of deposit, he has a negotiable instrument. The certificate, or confirmation that the deposit exists, is obtained from the bank with whom the deposit is made. This initial transaction takes place in the Primary CD Market.

The deposit remains a time deposit as far as the bank issuing the CD is concerned: it will only repay the money at the end of the agreed deposit period.

The Secondary CD Market

If the depositor wants his money, he can sell his CD, that is, his entitlement to the deposit, on the Secondary CD Market. Thus, a CD is a much more liquid asset than a simple corresponding Eurocurrency time deposit.

Selling, trading, or negotiating the certificate does not guarantee that exactly the same sum will be received as initially deposited. As the backing of the CD is a fixed period time deposit, this in itself will exert a 'pull to expiry of the deposit period repayment value' on the market price of the CD similar to the 'pull to redemption' effect on the price of redeemable gilts (see Chapter 1).

A comparison of the deposit rate colums in Table 9.2 shows exactly what theoretical considerations would suggest. The dollar CD rates are slightly less than the corresponding Eurodollar time deposit rates.

Table 9.2 A comparison of rates on Eurodollar time deposits and dollar certificates of Deposit

Time	Eurodollar deposit (%)	Dollar Certificate of Deposit
1 month	8.25 – 8.375	8.15 – 8.25
3 months	8.37 – 8.500	8.25 – 8.35
6 months	8.62 – 8.750	8.45 – 8.55
1 year	9.25 – 9.375	9.00 – 9.20

Source: *Financial Times*, 31 January 1985

The slightly higher (around 0.125%) rates on Eurodollar time deposits reflects the relative illiquidity of the deposit compared to the CD. A depositor has to wait until the end of the time indicated before his deposit is repaid whereas the CD holder has the more liquid asset and choice!

He could wait until the deposit period is up or get dollars at any time by trading his CD. The price he pays for this flexibility and liquidity lies in the lower interest rate paid on such deposits.

Certificates of deposit exist in other areas. A similar narrative to the one above could have been written about sterling CDs or ECU CDs. They also are not investments for the 'small man.' When they were originally introduced, they were in multiples of $25,000.

Notes

1 The Floating Rate Note(FRN) dates from 1970. Lenders would be more likely to commit funds for long periods if the rate of interest paid moved in line with market rates. Funds raised in this way amounted to $15bn in 1983. As an example, in December 1984, the International Bank for Reconstruction and Development raised a loan of Cdn $200,000,000 due December 2083, a 99 year Floating Rate Note. This sum probably could not have been raised on a fixed rate base except at very high rates unacceptable to the borrower. For more information, see 'The international market for floating-rate instruments', *Bank of England Quarterly Bulletin*, September 1984, Vol. 24, No. 3.

Consider the nature of the protection in this long lending of Canadian dollars to the International Bank for Reconstruction and Development. The bank will not repay for nearly one hundred years. The lenders will have made the loan from deposits repayable at varying terms but nothing like one hundred years. Thus, the risk is that the depositors will demand repayment at some time. As the floating rate on this loan moves in line with market rates, this will ensure the marketability of the note at anticipated prices regarded as satisfactory by the lenders. The rates charged on these notes are usually fixed in relationship to the LIBOR (London interbank offer rate).

2 'Requiem for the world's bankers postponed', *Economist*, 11 September 1982.

3 G. Cassel, 'Abnormal deviations in international exchange', *Economic Journal*, December 1918, pp. 413–15.

4 For more information, see W. P. Hogan and I. F. Pearce, *The Incredible Eurodollar*, Allen & Unwin, 1983.

Index